Dear Pitman Publishing Customer

IMPORTANT – Please Rea

We are delighted to announce a special free service
Simply complete this form and return it to the FREEPOST ad

A Free Customer Newsletter
B Free Information Service
C Exclusive Customer Offers – which have included free so
D Opportunity to take part in product development sessions
E The chance for you to write about your own business experience and become one of our respected authors

CW00428685

Fill this in now and return it to us (no stamp needed in the UK) to join our customer information service.

Name: Position:

Company/Organisation:

Address (including postcode):

Country:

Telephone: Fax:

Nature of business:

Title of book purchased:

ISBN (printed on back cover): [0] [2][7][3] [ ][ ][ ][ ] [ ]

Comments:

- | Fold Here Then Staple Once | -

We would be very grateful if you could answer these questions to help us with market research.

1 Where/How did you hear of this book?
[ ] in a bookshop
[ ] in a magazine/newspaper
(please state which):

[ ] information through the post
[ ] recommendation from a colleague
[ ] other (please state which):

2 Where did you buy this book
[ ] Direct from Pitman Publishing
[ ] From a bookclub
[ ] From a bookshop (state which)

3 Which newspaper(s)/magazine(s) do you read regularly?:

4 When buying a business book which factors influence you most?
(Please rank in order)
[ ] recommendation from a colleague
[ ] price
[ ] content
[ ] recommendation in a bookshop
[ ] author
[ ] publisher
[ ] title
[ ] other(s):

5 Is this book a
[ ] personal purchase?
[ ] company purchase?

6 Would you be prepared to spend a few minutes talking to our customer services staff to help with product development? YES/NO

PITMAN PUBLISHING

The Business Publisher

Written for managers competing in today's tough business world, our books will give you a competitive edge by showing you how to:

- increase quality, efficiency and productivity throughout your organisation
- use both proven and innovative management techniques
- improve your management skills and those of your staff
- implement winning customer strategies

In short they provide concise, practical information that you can use every day to increase the success of your business.

Free Information Service
Pitman Professional Publishing
FREEPOST
128 Long Acre
LONDON
WC2E 9BR, UK

No stamp
necessary
in the UK

How to be a Great Communicator

The Complete Guide to Mastering Internal Communication

■

DAVID M. MARTIN

the Institute
of Management

FOUNDATION

PITMAN
PUBLISHING

The Institute of Management (IM) is at the forefront of management development and best management practice. The Institute embraces all levels of management from students to chief executives. It provides a unique portfolio of services for all managers, enabling them to develop skills and achieve management excellence. If you would like to hear more about the benefits of membership, please write to Department P, Institute of Management, Cottingham Road, Corby NN17 1TT. This series is commissioned by the Institute of Management Foundation.

PITMAN PUBLISHING
128 Long Acre, London WC2E 9AN

A Division of Longman Group Limited

First published in Great Britain 1995

© David M. Martin 1995

British Library Cataloguing in Publication Data
A CIP catalogue record for this book can be obtained
from the British Library

ISBN 0 273 61262 X

1 3 5 7 9 10 8 6 4 2

Typeset by Northern Phototypesetting Co. Ltd, Bolton
Printed and bound in Great Britain by
Bell and Bain Ltd, Glasgow

*The Publisher's policy is to use paper manufactured
from sustainable forests.*

Contents

■

Contents

Introduction

■

This is my fourth book for this Institute of Management series. It was intended to be the first, but along the way its original outline was altered into that for the best-selling *Tough Talking*. *Tough Talking* sought to give guidance on the handling of awkward situations, showing how to better achieve one's aims by reviewing each person's desired result and altering one's own approach accordingly. *Manipulating Meetings* followed the same theme, applied to the particular circumstances of meetings; whilst *Dealing with Demanding Customers* used a similar approach to examine ways in which we can improve customer care and relationships.

Each of this book's predecessors has as its key, successful communication. Communication is a word which has become somewhat debased by over- and incorrect use. When we talk or write to another person, we often describe this as communicating with them, but this is not what we are doing. We may be informing them or giving them information, but that of itself is not communication. Only when the other party replies (that is, has an input) and demonstrates that they fully understand the item we have imparted to them, does a communication process begin.

Too often management, whose responsibility it is to foster internal communication, believe that by imparting information they are communicating. In this they delude themselves. They assume because they understand the message, that the recipient will. This may be so (although often it is not) but unless they then listen to what the recipient has to say about it, to query, and to gain additional explanation, no communicative process has taken place. Encouraging input from the recipient is essential before we can claim to be communicating.

$$C = I^2 \text{ (Communication equals information squared)}$$

To try to emphasise the difference between one-way information and two-way communication, we can perhaps use the power of 2 in the above definition. Like ripples on a pond spreading geometrically, communication encompasses a much wider 'area' than, for example, two items of information could encompass. It is a dynamic force involving, encouraging and incentivising. Information does none of these things well – if at all.

The essential two-way aspect of communication can be emphasised further by simply considering the word itself.

COMMUNICATION

Contains	2 'C's
	2 'O's
	2 'M's
	2 'N's
and	2 'T's

Only three letters appear singly. It is, in short, a very 'dual' word and so should its use be!

By inviting employees to participate in communication management can involve them in every aspect of the business, harnessing their ideas and suggestions for the good of the whole. The word 'incentivise' is used widely, and I have defined it in this book, as the process by which we encourage and motivate people so that they do willingly what we could alternatively force them to do. Tasks completed under threat are rarely, in my experience, performed as well as those which we want to do. This seems to me to be the point and purpose of trying to be a great communicator. This book provides many ideas and examples of how we can work towards this aim. However it must be realised that being a great communicator is not easy. It requires a great deal of constant practice and can be very time-consuming. The rewards however, as many of the true case studies included here describe, can be considerable. For everyone involved in management it is essential.

David M. Martin
Buddenbrook, November 1994

1

To lead, first communicate

'Once more unto the breach dear friends, once more'

Key learning points

1 'He who communicates leads' and he who wishes to lead must communicate – in the fullest sense of the word
2 Leadership is most effective relating directly with those at the sharp end – and so is communication
3 Most followers want to be led, directed *and* to be part of a communication process
4 Management's obligation is to lead – to manage, motivate and direct employees. To do this we need to communicate positively with them.

Apparently based on fact, Shakespeare has Henry V talking incognito to his men before the Battle of Agincourt in 1415. The king's purpose in adopting a disguise was to attempt to discover what his men really thought of both the forthcoming battle and of him. Disguised, his men will be unable to recognise him, and thus, he correctly reasons, they are likely to be more truthful than they would be were he to ask the same questions as their king and commander, and by his appearance condition them to temper their words.

One soldier tells him 'ay he [the king] said so in order to make us fight cheerfully' – aptly summing up the whole point of the king's rallying calls, such as his address to his men on the eve of battle which Shakespeare paraphrased in the classic 'breach' speech. Henry knew that incentivising (that is encouraging and motivating people so that they act willingly) his small force was essential if it were to face the foe. His exhortations were so effective, that, following the storming and capture of the fortress town of Harfleur, the tiny army went on to win a resounding victory at Agincourt. That victory was remarkable since it was won against a vastly superior force (the French army was four times the size of Henry's) fighting on its home territory, while Henry and his men had just marched over 250 miles in 17 days, and they and their rations were almost exhausted.

Victory – V

Agincourt was won, like Poitiers and Crécy, and countless other battles before and since, largely by the cohesive effect of good commanders, communicating with and leading their men from the front. Having said that, the considerable contribution made by the fiercely effective English longbow must not be overlooked. It is said that the French opponents threatened that if they caught English archers, they would amputate their index and third fingers so they would be unable to 'knock', or position, an arrow on a bowstring. As a means of intimidating their enemy thereafter, the English used to hold aloft those fingers indicating that they were still effective archers, and a force to be reckoned with. This legend is said to be the origination of the famed 'V-sign'. Five hundred years after Agincourt, a twentieth-century leader adapted that sign to indicate both victory for his country and country-folk, and a similar derision and defiance to their modern-day enemies to that evinced by Agincourt's archers. Churchill's two fingers held aloft were a sign that everyone could understand, relate to and use. It symbolised, by means of its widespread use, a working together in a common purpose to achieve a common end – in this case the defeat of an enemy.

Communication can thus appear in many forms – in words, in deeds and in signs, and in attempting to become great communicators we need to use whichever is appropriate to the particular occasion.

The ultimate aim

The Second World War of 1939–45 was eventually won in Europe, following the invasion of Normandy in 1944 by the Allied Expeditionary Force, under its supreme commander, General Eisenhower, who, like Churchill, well understood the need to bolster morale by communicating with those under his command to attain an ultimate aim. He spent a great deal of time visiting and talking to the troops in over 1,000 of their encampments. To the British, reared on formality and the rigid rules of class relationships, Eisenhower's informal and self-effacing style was refreshing. Like Napoleon before him, of whom his eventual victor Wellington said, 'his presence on the field made the difference of forty thousand men', Eisenhower's presence gave an immediate boost to morale, and his ready smile was said to be worth 20 divisions in the field.

The common touch

To lead his land forces Eisenhower chose Field Marshal Montgomery who himself had a highly individual method of operating. In addition to his normal chain of command he utilised liaison officers to discover exactly what was happening in each field of operation. After seeing, at first hand, how the battle was going, these liaison officers were able to brief their commander directly, informally and objectively. They became an extension of Montgomery's own eyes, ears and brain. With a force of around 5,000, it was possible for Henry V to address all his soldiers, or at least be seen in person by them, and for him to gain first-hand experience of their views and to incentivise them directly.

3

With a force of over 100 times the size of Henry's, coincidentally fighting over the same land, Montgomery needed additional eyes and ears to tell him 'how it really was', and to guide his actions and strategy. While the reaction of senior officers to Monty's liaison officers was not always positive, as they regarded them, with some justification, as spying on them, their own junior officers usually regarded them as valuable allies. Those junior officers knew that there was more than a possibility that their own views and questions would reach the ears of their commander, rather than being filtered out by those between. Monty himself would also make frequent and informal visits to his men in the field, with the field marshal, although a non-smoker himself, handing round cigarettes to his men. As Abraham Lincoln had said around 100 years earlier, 'if you would win a man to your cause, first convince him you are his sincere friend'. The easy relationship of such leaders with those at the sharp end, often referred to as 'the common touch', requires the gift of perception, which enables those that possess it to assess, with a reasonable degree of accuracy, how their followers really think and feel. Such leaders invariably seek to support such semi-intuitive beliefs through first-hand evidence encouraging feedback to check their beliefs. In doing so, by means of face-to-face meetings, discussions and, above all, listening, they achieve true communication as well as actively motivating their followers.

Creating the extraordinary response

Throughout history there are countless examples of deeds of valour achieved or victories won, often in the face of overwhelming odds, by ordinary people responding to the demands of extraordinary circumstances, and performing acts of courage and dedication. Such acts are not necessarily performed in the heat of the battle or in the immediate face of the enemy. The spirit of Londoners during the Blitz of the same war, despite immense hardships and suffering, played an important part in maintaining the morale of the country. Here both Churchill and another king (George VI) played a vital part in sustaining morale.

4

Case study 1.1
PUTTING IT INTO PERSPECTIVE

On visiting an engineering works, George VI, who remained in London despite pressure to move to Canada for the duration, found employees in good heart although apparently unaware of the importance of the locking nuts they were producing. In fact the nuts were used as part of the fastening of propellers to the aircraft the country was desperately trying to produce, and whose output was critical to the winning of the Battle of Britain. When the king discovered their ignorance, he insisted that the staff were told. It is said that output increased considerably because the employees then understood the vital importance of their task.

Key technique
Basically people cannot care about something that they do not know or understand. The more people care, the more committed they will be to the aims of the endeavour. Perhaps communication could be defined as a process that helps people understand and care in order to tie their efforts closely to the ultimate aims.

On a much smaller scale the BBC television programme *999* features reconstructions of real-life emergencies. While its aim is in part to demonstrate the professionalism of the emergency services, the series also features numerous instances where bystanders, sometimes entirely lacking the benefit of the professionals' training, equipment and knowledge, and acting in a way dictated often by little more than perceived common sense, often perform, with little regard for their own safety, feats of considerable courage.

In most cases, in both national and local emergencies, the majority of people have the capacity to perform acts and deeds which in ordinary circumstances they might not consider within their capabilities or be prepared to contemplate. Often their reasoning for so acting is 'there was no one else around so I had to do it'. With this reaction we need to ask ourselves, why so often, in so many industrial and commercial organisations, is there an unwillingness to perform at such high standards or with such dedication?

Peer pressure

One answer seems to be that if there are several people present, there can be a general 'holding back', with each waiting for someone else to make the first move, a reticence which may not be felt by the sole onlooker. Individual action results from a personal initiative, but overcoming the inertia of the many requires leadership qualities and above all communication akin to that displayed by those who, like Henry V, lead from the front. While the sole helper may be incentivised to action by the fact that the onus is very much on him or her, when action is required by the many, we need someone to be a focal point, to incentivise, to organise and, above all, to communicate in order to lead.

The brilliant victories at Agincourt which won control of France by the English crown and Normandy which led to the freeing of Europe from the grip of the Nazis are half a millennium apart, and each are light years away from each other and from a young man swimming across miles of ice-cold water to bring help to his injured friends, or a doctor tunnelling into a collapsed building and risking her own life to aid a trapped child. Yet each provide lessons. The common thread between Henry V and George VI, between Churchill, Eisenhower and Montgomery, was that they understood people and, furthermore, that they understood that most people need to be understood, to be motivated and to be directed to achieve the ultimate end. In short, people need to be involved by means of communication, and by communication means if they are to be led, and to achieve the desired result. Some, like those that act in emergencies when others only stand immobilised, may be able to motivate and 'lead' themselves. Most organisations need both types of person and a meld of both, directed by a person with vision and purpose, should generate an effective team. The critical ingredient – the catalyst – is that of the communicating leader. The leader must have vision, purpose, and the ability to relate to and motivate his or her team. What is perhaps so sad is the fact that whereas we seem able to rise to the challenge of the disaster (like Agincourt or D-Day) or the emergency (even when this occurs in company), we often seem unable to deal effectively with the challenge of the everyday and the mundane. If we can win the 'war' so well, how is it that we so often fail to win the peace?

Case study 1.2
DIVIDED WE FALL

The company had been experiencing a period of several weeks of unhappy and increasingly partisan industrial relations arguments. This seemingly became compounded by the national imposition of a three-day working week. However the imposition, because of a national strike by coal miners, of statutory controls and prohibitions regarding the use of power on 'non-power' days, forced a reassessment of the previously entrenched positions regarding demarcation issues. Almost instantly the old arguments were put aside, and management and unions worked in harmony to try to ensure productive output, and the capacity to earn wages was maintained.

Key technique
External threats may provide an impetus to join together in order to defeat the common 'foe'.

Case study 1.3
CARELESSNESS

In the late 1980s and early 1990s the UK suffered a number of highly publicised tragedies. In each case there were examples of courage and leadership from those dealing with the results of such tragedies. Ironically, it seemed to many outsiders that often the terrible misery and suffering could have been avoided had attention been paid to the basic means of operation of the organisations affected.

Key technique
Basic procedures and rules need to be in place (and adequately communicated to all involved) before we can consider improving commitment and involvement. An effective communication programme may also be helpful in improving such guidelines – few people understand the real situation as well as those at the sharp end.

In both these examples, the imposition of an outside event forced a reassessment of the basics. In the company, the very real and imminent possibility of it failing due to circumstances over which it had no control, forced a reassessment of priorities. The issues which had formerly seemed so vital were thrust into perspective and sublimated in favour of more urgent considerations. Both sides 'agreed' to forget their own internal differences in order to fight the common enemy. Following the various national tragedies, rules and guidelines were implemented which brought basic requirements to the forefront of everyone's attention.

Case study 1.4
GAINING ATTENTION – THE HARD WAY

The school had been built over 25 years previously on a quiet road. Due to poor planning decisions and changes of two bus routes, the road past the school was now busy, congested and dangerous. For some time parents and school had been campaigning for the creation of lay-bys to alleviate some of the congestion and potential danger, but without a great deal of success. Then a young child was knocked down by a manoeuvring vehicle and within two months of that accident being given publicity, the lay-bys were completed and the congestion relieved.

Key technique
Communication can be very hard to achieve particularly when there are some committed to frustrate it or to blur the situation.

7

Removing the blur

Faced with emergencies akin to those problems faced by Henry V at Agincourt or Montgomery in Northern France, or the management and union with the three-day week, the eventual aim may be clear-cut. When such an event occurs, often the person in the hot seat can immediately perceive that the all-important priority is to stop the bleeding, save the life, preserve the company or, in other words, to win their particular 'war'. Faced with an emergency their desired result and their ultimate aim may be clear-cut and unequivocal. Further, such aims, hopefully obvious to those in control and with responsibility, can be underlined by their urgings, to try to gain at least tacit agreement from those less committed to the ultimate aim. However, when the ultimate problem is not so threatening to life or the quality of life such ultimate aims can become blurred. Blurring can be caused as much by an abundance of choice as by a lack of comprehension of the ultimate aim.

Faced with a marauding enemy, many will fight to the death to protect home and kin, but lacking such an external threat, what would then be held so dear may be taken for granted and even lost.

The company faced with failure and extinction by the imposition of the three-day week, constantly faced such problems in attempting to outperform competition, maintain quality, and achieve competitive prices and service. The fact that these were everyday problems did not make them any less real, but it took the imposition of a threat by an external force, to bring such problems into focus. During the briefings that became part of the joint initiative to ensure survival, many employees were heard to comment that they had not previously realised how slim was the margin between success and failure, particularly for a company without immediate access to extra cash in times of slack output or productivity. The explaining of such economic facts of life to the workforce to garner their whole-hearted commitment to the flexible arrangements aimed at ensuring survival was instrumental in bringing about a sea-change of attitudes to such matters as materials usage, quality and delivery times. Explaining how costs and delays affected profits, and thus the security of their own jobs, made the employees *care*.

The campaigners for improved road safety near the school had lobbied the council, their member of parliament and other authorities involved, but had not been able to gain a tenth of the attention achieved by the press when it featured the accident involving the child. Their activities had been blurred (and blunted) by the opposing actions of those not so committed to their aims. In leading, in commanding, in setting goals or aims, we need to remove any blur, and promulgate clear messages and purpose – we must communicate in the widest sense of the word. Unfortunately, all too often our efforts can be negated by the activities of those who are motivated by self-preservation – like Monty's senior officers, or the council officials who, rather than deal with a road safety problem, indulged in time-wasting correspondence. If we wish to become a great communicator we must recognise and remove all such obstacles.

The enemy

While it may be somewhat emotive to consider the problems connected with and advantages to be derived from communication in terms of war and battles, when here we are concerned with organisations in peace, nevertheless with increased globalisation of markets and competition, our commercial opponents can pose dangers to our organisations similar to those of a marauding enemy to its opponents. The competitors of our profit-making organisation will have, as their aim, gaining an advantage which, if they are successful, could lead ultimately to the closure or 'death' of our organisation. In these circumstances, the commitment of those involved in the survival of the organisation is every bit as essential as those fighting for survival in the London Blitz. Those who withstood such incessant pounding had little choice: they either had to fight back or give in and die, or at least see their way of life die. It may be difficult for those not at the sharp end of business, not conversant with or given financial data about it, or who do not interface with customers to understand that unless they do their work to the best of their ability the success of their employing organisation will be blunted. This was a fact that the employees of the company facing closure because of the imposition of the three-day week found out almost too late.

9

Understanding that profit-making organisations cannot stand still – they must either expand and live, or else contract and ultimately die – is the message that needs to be put across, particularly in the ultra-competitive 1990s, when everyone is and will be trying to gain a larger slice of a smaller cake or at the very least to hold on to the slice they have. This is not to say that this is an easy task – in many cases it will pose considerable difficulties. However, the benefits are that those responsible for achieving the results required of the organisation should have a clearer idea of how they can help attain those aims. In turn this will lead to a situation where the aims of the individuals are more closely aligned to the aims of the organisations for which they work, to their mutual benefit.

Case study 1.5
3,000 SALES REPRESENTATIVES

In endeavouring to improve quality and delivery, the director during his briefings on the financial results involving nearly all employees, suggested that they all think of themselves as sales representatives. This had some success – particularly among those dealing with the storage and delivery of finished stock. Losses from customer returns halved after the effect on sales of the customers being given damaged outers of products was explained. At the next round of such briefings, the director enlisted the help of a sales representative who explained her problems in trying to sell to a customer whose previous order had been subject to quality problems. The recounting of real-life problems (including the (unprintable) remarks made by several customers) brought home to those responsible the effect of their own poor work in a way that no memo or poster could have achieved. Their own suggestions and input were then sought to improve the situation. Within three months, quality problems had halved and so had material losses.

Key technique
Communicating the problem can encourage commitment, but without relating it to the individual, little may be achieved. There is little to lose in endeavouring to capture commitment, but potentially a great return. Communicating in this sense is of course far more than just telling everyone of the problem as is highlighted in Chapter 2.

The doubtful allies

In recent years there has been a growth in fashionable excursions aimed at helping organisations lead, motivate and communicate with their employees. While there is little doubt that retaining experts to assist in particular areas can be very effective, there is a danger of delegating to such experts, the duties and responsibilities, primarily of communication, that properly belong to the organisation's leader. Ideally, top level leadership should be holistic – an entity. It should not be dissected and delegated; motivation should not be divided into tranches to be administered by separate individuals; communication with those involved should not be cascaded, so that by the time the message hits those for whom it was intended, 50 per cent of the effect has been lost.

It has been said that the most effective organisation may be the sole trader. The sole trader has total control over all aspects of his or her operation. A sole trader has no need to communicate their aims as they know them and can concentrate their attention on achieving them. Once the sole trader takes on one extra person however, the leadership, motivation, communication challenge is on. That additional person needs to have the aims of the business explained to them and to be motivated to move the business forward to attain that aim – not just once but constantly, since the business will be constantly altering. This need to communicate effectively is an essential part of management. The sole trader may find, as a result of the additional commitment in this area, that his or her own direct efforts are somewhat blunted, which is acceptable assuming the efforts of the extra individual more than compensate. However, essentially the sole trader has moved away from a 'doing' job towards a 'directing' job. Unfortunately some of those used to performing a 'doing' job never truly master the move to the requirements of a 'directing' job.

Case study 1.6
'DON'T BOTHER ME, I'M BUSY'

The accounting manager was responsible for a staff of 15. Unfortunately, in promoting him to his present job, the board had insisted that he retained direct responsibility for the preparation of the monthly accounts package which absorbed at least 75 per cent of his time. His subordinates dealt with a whole range of accounting responsibilities, but received little guidance from him, since he was usually too preoccupied doing his 'own work'. His perceived priority was the work for which he had direct responsibility, although as a manager of 15 people his real priority should have been the management and direction of those staff, delegating some of his own tasks in the process.

Often his reaction to a staff problem was 'Oh, pop down to Personnel and get them to sort it out', to an organisational problem, 'Can't you get Organisation and Methods to see to it?', and even to an accounting problem 'Ask the auditors'.

Key technique
Had the manager been able to give his staff adequate time, to communicate with them and to really manage their activities, he would have provided leadership, support and assistance to them. Instead there was a void – a situation made worse by a rising turnover of staff in the department.

11

While 'staff' functions, such as personnel, organisation and methods, training (and even the auditors), can play a valuable role, essentially their purpose is to assist, not to substitute for, effective person-management. The best manager of personnel is (or should be) the line manager: no one should know his or her staff better, and no one should have more time to control, communicate with and motivate his or her staff than their own manager. No one should use more resources communicating and interpreting the aims of the business and their own department to ensure the attainment of a common purpose. Indeed, no true manager or leader should want the input of an outsider, even though they should be prepared to listen to, and even use, their advice.

Communication/leadership guidelines

- Build the team and work to make it achieve the results.

- Clearly define and set the task (in completely unambiguous and clear language), and coach and support those required to achieve it.

- Manage (that is support, coach, train, develop) the team members.

- Talk to and listen to each member of the team.

- Delegate (or empower) to as great an extent as possible so that you can stand back, plan for the future and manage the team members.

- Discuss problems, and use suggestions and ideas from those involved.

- Use organisation charts to demonstrate relationships without letting them become strait jackets.

- Outlaw demarcation disputes.

- Draw solutions from those at the sharp end rather than imposing solutions on them.

- Be visible, approachable and patient.

Once wonders what Henry V, Churchill and Montgomery, with their instinctive grasp of how to handle and lead their followers, would have made of the suggestion that management and leadership decisions properly theirs should be made by outsiders. The campaign that culminated in the splendid victory at Agincourt might have turned out somewhat differently if Henry V had asked his aide-de-camp to 'do' his 'breach speech'. Leadership is about personal example, about clarity of vision, about motivating people – and to achieve all of it the leader needs to communicate clearly, continually and adequately.

·2

Consistent communication

'Girding the loins'

Key learning points

1 Whilst external initiatives may assist, true two-way communication with those involved will solve most problems
2 Responsibility for communication is 'firmly pinned to the chest of every manager'
3 Information is not communication and the two must be clearly differentiated
4 Leadership and communication are best achieved when the parties meet face to face and regularly

13

Organisations have only two tangible assets – money to be manipulated and people to be motivated. Sadly, on too many occasions, it seems that it is employees who are manipulated and money is the only motivation. Statements such as 'employees are our greatest asset' are enunciated without much more than lip-service being paid to the true meaning and implications of the phrases. Yet its employees are the greatest asset of any organisation, since without their effort and work nothing whatever can be achieved. If this is not as widely understood as it should be, the fact that good quality, trained and committed employees can improve the perception and performance of the organisation as much as poor quality and poorly motivated employees can mar and blunt it, is even more poorly realised. The solution is simple. The need is to generate commitment to the organisation so that employees understand:

■ what their employer is trying to do;
■ how their efforts and jobs contribute to the business, and how they can help; and

- how and why decisions need to be made, and made the way they are.

This takes communication and leadership, and if all organisations have two assets, it can be argued that the best and often most successful organisations have one further asset – that of quality leadership. The gift of leadership is often what separates the good performer from the best. In *Managing your Internal Customers* (Financial Times/Pitman Publishing 1993), Kevin Thomson lists a number of well-known companies highly regarded for their positive images. For the image of 'staff care' Marks & Spencer was nominated. It is surely no coincidence that the company, well known for its employee relationships, is also the UK's premier retailer. Not only do good leaders have clear views of their priorities and sublimate personal ambitions in the interest of the greater good of the organisation, but also in order to lead they communicate every aspect of their vision, their standards and their requirements. Where such leadership is absent, it is possible that we can substitute for it in other ways, although rarely will this be as effective.

In 1944 Montgomery had around half a million men under his control, with less than 10 per cent in positions of authority or the equivalent of 'management'. This compares with the employment profile found in many organisations in the post industrial revolution period. Until recently wealth-producing bodies tended to utilise large numbers of employees at the 'sharp end', directed by relatively few managers. Many of these 'foot soldiers' carried out boring, repetitive tasks, often linked to machine processes, which required little positive motivation. 'Keep your head down and do as you are told' tended to be a widespread attitude. While this may have been understandable (it is difficult to believe it is ever acceptable), until, say the early 1960s in the UK, increasingly both the response of the shop floor and the balance of skills required by such organisations have changed.

The UK education system for the past 20 years – at least in theory – has encouraged pupils to question, to challenge and to be more assertive. As the products of such a system move into employment, similar attitudes will become more widespread in employment. Increasingly people are not prepared to keep quiet and obey orders. They may be prepared to carry out instructions but require explanations and even justification. The key is motivation – an internal force which makes employees put real effort and energy into the tasks required of them, to contribute to the better performance of such tasks, and to work willingly and with purpose.

14

Communication guidelines to ensure motivation

- Individual recognition – known by name.

- Treatment as a responsible human being.

- Well led to clearly defined aims and tasks.

- Involvement in planning and improving work processes.

- Work, output and performance monitored, and coaching provided.

- Assistance/guidance available when required.

- Praised as well as criticised when appropriate.

- Encouraged to take on more responsibility.

- Regular reviews of progress utilised.

- Informal structure.

15

Properly motivated, employees should carry out their duties more willingly and constructively than those subjected to the 'mushroom management' of the past. (Mushroom management entails people being kept in the dark and having muck piled on top of them.)

Employment changes

Seemingly ever more rapidly changing technological advances mean that fewer 'foot soldiers', that is the unskilled or those with a low level of skills, are needed. Following extensive research, leading consultants McKinsey estimate that, by the year 2000, 70 per cent of all European jobs will require professional skills (that is A levels or higher), while the remaining 30 per cent will require skills only marginally less. The Confederation of British Industry (CBI), commenting on this research, stressed that 'outstanding communication skills' will be needed by these employees. Equally outstanding communication skills will be needed in order to deal with them. For every manager, becoming a great communicator is already a challenge needing to be addressed as a matter of considerable urgency.

This preparedness to question is also beginning to find its way into our customers' relationships with suppliers. The British were always said to put up with poor quality and poor service without complaining;

not wishing to 'make a fuss' they prefer to vote with their feet. Not any more: we now have a younger generation ready to question and an older generation with considerable purchasing power. The lesson of the recession of the early 1990s is that consumers are actively seeking value for money. This attitude will increasingly be found in-company. The days of 'mushroom management' are numbered – employees will increasingly demand openness, explanations and being kept updated.

BS 5750 et al

Partly in recognition of this changing employment profile, there have recently been a succession of initiatives designed to assist the effectiveness of management of employees. While in no way undermining or belittling the success of these initiatives where they have worked well, we should perhaps question the basis of their success, as one cannot help but wonder if such success may be attributed, not so much to the particular characteristics of each individual scheme, but to a conduit which is underlying and common to all, as follows.

- BS 5750 (the quality standard now to be known by the ultra-snappy title, BS EN ISO 9000) seeks to provide a means by which quality of production, output and service in an organisation is instituted and/or improved.
- Total Quality Management (TQM) is basically a means of moving towards, through and beyond BS 5750, applying its precepts in all its forms and at all levels in an organisation.
- Empowerment initiatives seek to encourage employees to consider their operations and their part in the organisation, and to encourage them to play a more positive role, to take on responsibility.
- The principles developed by the Investors in People initiative seek to involve and develop all employees within an organisation to improve productivity and output, and to reduce waste.
- Process re-engineering requires the involvement of employees in reconsidering the way in which their employer is organised in order to improve systems, procedures, output and quality, etc.

and so on.

While it is true that aspects of each may be original and novel, and might not work without the adoption of the rules and requirements of the individual initiative, where each has been successful, surely this is more related to the fact that, in order to introduce each, management are actually having to do what they are always supposed to do – leading, talking and listening to their employees? Indeed, it must be arguable that if only management had really communicated with their employees adequately, comprehensively and consistently in the first place, they might not have needed to embrace the initiatives at all. The director in case study 2.4 had not heard of BS 5750 (indeed his initiative predated it), Investors in People or employee empowerment. He simply reasoned that if people were treated as adults, encouraged to understand the problems and to accept that there was something that they could individually do about them, then their own common sense would do the rest – as indeed it did. Writing in *Involvement* (the journal of the Involvement and Participation Association) in August 1994, Anthony Barry commented 'it is significant that organisations which have made major strides in employee involvement seem to have made progress in empowerment, whilst those sticking to "managements' right to manage" have encountered the biggest problems'.

However, if the only way in which we can encourage managers to actively communicate with their staff in order to motivate them is via the conduit of a nationally accepted and accredited initiative – then do it by all means. It is certainly better than nothing – providing bureaucracy does not impair effectiveness.

17

Case study 2.1
THE HAWTHORNE INVESTIGATIONS

For several years from the mid 1920s, a number of lighting experiments were carried out at the Hawthorne Works, Chicago, of the Western Electric Company. It was believed that improved lighting increased output, so two groups were set up – an experimentation group and a control group (which continued working as normal). The lighting for the working area occupied by the experimental group was improved and its output increased; the lighting was reduced and the output increased. The manner in which the work was organised was changed and the output increased. Then, when the employees were allowed to set their own working pattern and organisation, the output achieved its highest rate. Even when the lighting was decreased to such an extent that the light was akin to the intensity of moonlight, no fall from the previous improved levels was registered.

But what of the control group? In the control group nothing had been changed and yet its output also rose. In fact, of course, it is incorrect to state that nothing had changed. The control group knew that they were part of the experiment, despite their working conditions being left unaltered.

Key technique
In both groups, the fact that they had been recognised by management as suitable for experiment itself worked as a motivating force. When the experiments were ceased, output fell away again and, when asked why, one of the participants is said to have commented 'We had lost our self-respect'.

Carrying the day

Only if someone communicates well can they be a good leader and experience indicates that the best leaders automatically tend to be good communicators. Indeed, it may be that *because* they are good communicators they rise to become leaders. Good leaders instinctively realise that they can only achieve their aims by carrying others with them. To carry along their followers requires them to interface with such followers. Interfacing with the employees at the Hawthorne Works brought immediate, if somewhat unexpected, benefits, particularly from those employees apparently not involved in the experiments. Leadership is not about having a chairman or chairwoman (henceforth chairman) – most organisations will have such a person, even though their exact title may vary. But not everyone with such a title is a communicating leader and, if they are not, it is unlikely either that clear aims have been set for the organisation or that those working there are motivated to give of their best in the attainment of such aims. Leadership can be defined as directing by example – we may lead best by being, like Henry V, in the van of the fight. Our presence at the sharp end shows we are committed to our own aims and are prepared to share the difficulties of those actually engaged in the business to attain those aims. Indeed, in doing so we are virtually forced to communicate in order to survive. Sadly, often those who perceive themselves as leaders, attempt to direct without first-hand knowledge, without feedback and without perception of the real views of their 'foot soldiers'.

In attempting to discover his men's real views, and in leading from the front, Henry V had two powerful weapons – knowledge and example. Conversely, the leadership of the British army in the 1914–18 war received considerable criticism since so often it seemed they were directing activities from a safe rear position, a situation which could only lead to antagonism and irritation of those left to do the fighting, whose high morale was critical. 'Lions led by donkeys' was the phrase used to describe that army. While it can be argued that the intellects and skills best able to direct the campaign need protection and should not be exposed to unnecessary danger, it may be difficult to instil the essential morale and commitment at the sharp end, if so-called leaders are never seen sharing the hardships of those at the sharp end.

Case study 2.2
FIRING MOTIVATES

The factory was located in the West Country of England, an area with considerable unemployment. When the decision to close it down was taken by its parent company 300 miles away, it was decided to provide an on-the-spot outplacement service. Over the following six months, the appointee visited the factory every week to help the redundant employees find alternative work. However, he swiftly realised that many of the problems of poor output that had led to the closure decision were actually related to poor management and motivation rather than to lack of marketability of the products. During the project morale considerably increased, despite the workforce being under notice. As morale increased, so too did factory output, despite repeated loss of production time as employees attended interviews and spent time discussing their problems. In the six months from the serving of the notice of closure output, after an initial dip, attained record levels. The consultant's office was on the factory floor, with glass walls, so he could both see and be seen.

The on-site management carried on with their work, from an office remote from the factory floor, which was visited by them only two or three times a day.

Fortunately, as well as the 25 per cent for whom alternative jobs were found, a buyer was found for part of the business, thus saving the jobs of a further 45 per cent of the staff. The output figures attained played a part in convincing the buyer to invest.

Key technique:
When the consultant finished his assignment, many of the employees came to thank him for his help. 'I'm not sure I was that successful' he replied, 'there are still around 30 per cent of you who will be unemployed and who have little chance of finding jobs.' 'But you were one of us, listening to our problems. You gave us a pride in ourselves – no one seemed to bother before,' was the reply.

19

Remote 'leadership'

The lesson of remote leadership (which is a complete contradiction of terms), such as was epitomised by the British army in the 1914–18 war, seemed learned in 1939–45, when commanders were often seen at the front, interfacing with the men who would actually do the fighting. In business today, it is sad and reprehensible that some senior management still emulate the senior command of the First World War. There have been several instances where, despite redundancies being effected to reduce the number of sharp end personnel, top management have awarded themselves pay rises considerably in excess of the rate of inflation. In one classic instance huge payouts were made to top management leaving a company, having been responsible for incurring a massive loss. Writing in the *Mail on Sunday* in August 1994, former cabinet minister Alan Clark commented on this subject, 'there is a cosy clique at the top of corporate Britain whose first concern is to feather their own nests. The shareholders come second. The employees come last.'

How one can win the hearts and minds of those one is supposed to be leading in this situation is totally baffling – it seems as far removed from leading by example as is possible to achieve. It is interesting that in Japan, where generally productivity far exceeds that of the UK, and employees seem far better motivated, the differential between the pay of top managers and shop floor employees is much less than is the case generally in the UK – and particularly as is the case in some recently privatised industries.

There is an urgent need for leadership by example and a sharing of experiences in organisations to engender morale and commitment to the aims set by those responsible. This then generates a challenge to find ways and means by which such example can be conveyed through the organisation, to ensure that everyone is aware of the aims and that their efforts are geared to the attainment of those aims, and not to some personal and secret agenda.

The commitment conduit

What leadership needs to seek to achieve is a 'pulling together' of different people in the interests of the 'common cause' – as did management and unions when faced with the possibility of the loss of the company due to the imposition of the three-day week in case study 1.2. We can only achieve this 'pulling together' (in the absence of an external threat) through active, consistent and meaningful communication, and to do so, we need to appreciate the exact nature of the beast we wish to ride and to tame. It has been said that 'He who communicates, leads' – and conversely that he who would lead must communicate. Communication is not a science to be learned (even though its quality may be capable of improvement by the study of techniques and methods), since it is ingrained in every animal. We communicate with others throughout our life, from the baby crying to attract attention for food or warmth, to the teacher attempting to instil information into the brains or skills into the hands of pupils, to the politician trying to woo voters to give him or her power, and so on.

Homo sapiens is a communicative creature – and in our ordinary life, if we want something, we tend to communicate automatically and directly in order to obtain it. As a race we have developed very sophisticated methods by which we can communicate with apparently ever-increasing ease. Unfortunately it seems that sometimes we are so dazzled by the brilliance of the technology we overlook the fact that the simplest and often the most effective means of communication is that of simply talking face to face to our target audience. Indeed, very often the more sophisticated the means of communication, the less effective may be the imparting and discussion of the message itself. Senior management issued guidance notes, memos and budgets to the employees in case study 2.2 – but nothing was as effective as a regular interface on the shop floor, even though this was carried out by an outsider. Indeed, one could argue that, with a workforce of largely unsophisticated employees, the provision of sophisticated data is counter-productive and an informal interface will always be more effective.

After all, if we are face to face with a person we can use body language to emphasise our points far more effectively than underlining in a memo or bold type in a report, etc. Words can trap our message and reduce it to a mere shadow of itself – Henry V's 'breach speech' is infinitely more effective when we hear it spoken than when we read it ourselves from the page.

The onus on management

It is perhaps a sad reflection on UK management that the quotation 'he who communicates, leads' comes from Jack Jones who, when general secretary of the Transport and General Workers Union, set his aims out clearly and led his 'employees', his union members, towards the achievement of their aims with considerable success. It is also sad that, at that time, many employees received more information from, and engaged in more communication with, their unions than with their employers.

Case study 2.3
WHOSE RESPONSIBILITY?

The newly appointed communications manager was threading his way through the lunchtime crowds in the canteen, balancing his lunch tray, when he met a colleague whom he had known in a previous position. 'Hello, Peter' the colleague chirped, 'still communicating like mad?'

Key technique
He'd missed the point entirely. It is not – and never has been – the job of specialist communicators, whether in-house or consulting, personally to carry through the company's job of communication. That task is firmly pinned to the chest of every manager in the business.

From Peter Jackson's Corporate Communication for Managers, Pitman Publishing 1987

Such abdication of the responsibility for communicating with employees to trade union or personnel specialists may be on the decrease, as increasingly management, following a few excellent examples, have begun to realise the value of gaining commitment, involving and motivating employees as well as treating them as thinking, rational people, rather than as cogs in a machine, and have developed systems to help this movement. There is a tremendous opportunity for management to ensure it gains its employees' commitment by means of regular, dependable and accurate information, which itself will generate feedback and dialogue, since only when there is feedback will true two-way communication (as opposed to the essentially one-way flow that is the purveying of information) be generated.

Communication: the misunderstood process

The CBI underlined the above points when it stated in the late 1980s that 'effective communication with employees will be one of the major issues facing management over the next decade'. The CBI did not mean the dissemination of information which is essentially a one-way process, but a true two-way dialogue. If A tells B that the production target for this week is 1,000 widgets, that is information, which, although it is essential, in no way involves B or gains any commitment from him. However, if A sits down with B, asks him what manpower he has available, whether there are adequate supplies of raw material and power, and whether there are any problems in attaining the week's production target, and listens to the answers, and then they jointly decide a course of action, that is true communication at work. Communication is essentially a meeting of minds and a gaining of consensus, and from it is derived leadership and motivation. The person who initiates the communication and the discussion tends to become the leader; the respondent tends to be motivated by the other. If a leader is only as good as his or her followers, followers can only ever be as good as their leaders.

23

A two-way dialogue

True communication is essentially a two-way dialogue involving comprehension of both parties' viewpoint, concerns and priorities by the other. Comprehension is essential before communication exists and this can only be achieved by an exchange of information – that is it requires a dynamic, not a passive, process as Figure 2.1 tries to demonstrate.

Being an active rather than a passive process, communication requires both dedication to a long-term process and an understanding of the other party's viewpoint. Indeed, it requires an appreciation that until both sides really understand what the other means, messages can be confused and misunderstood. Thus, to be a great communicator, we *must* not just listen to what is being said, but also 'hear' what is or is not being said. This takes time and practice. 'The reason', goes the old saying, 'that we have one mouth and two ears, is that we can listen twice as much as we talk'. Sadly the opposite tends to be more often the case. Further, the passive state of hearing is all too often mistaken for active listening. The manager who claims proudly to talk to his or her employees regularly may be more to be admired than one who does not, but this is *not* communication. True communication will only occur when there is consensus about the subject matter, even if there is no agreement. 'Agreeing to differ' infers that at least the two sides may have understood each other's viewpoint. To foster true communication, all parties must be prepared to listen – actively and continually. It is easy to dissemble when the dialogue is only a two or three-sentence conversation, but far more difficult to conceal one's true attitude if the conversation is prolonged.

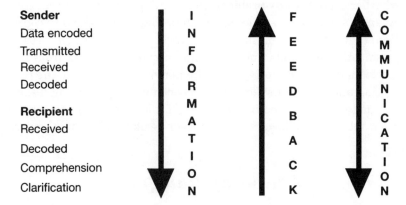

Figure 2.1 Information =/= communication

For this reason the 'walking the job' initiative (or as it has alternatively been titled 'management by wandering around') so inspiringly promoted by John Garnett when director of the Industrial Society in the 1970s and 1980s, while essential, can only work effectively when it is a regular process. Referring, in the annual report, to employees as 'our greatest asset' while ignoring their need for constant communication and motivation for the rest of the year is worse than completely ignoring them in the report. Such omission is at least consistent and does not generate feelings of hypocrisy. Similarly 'walking the job' means much more than Number 1 touring the units once a year for a photo-call for the report. The publication of such a photo on the shop floor may fool outsiders but it will fool no one internally – it can only indicate the hypocrisy of such an organisation and may actually be the source of demotivation.

Case study 2.4
WALKING THE JOB

The factory was in disarray – output was 50 per cent below budget, labour turnover was in excess of 100 per cent, and product quality was extremely variable. It was a complex operation beyond the capability of its previous manager who resigned a few days ahead of dismissal. The divisional chairman took control, and for the next three months he and his personnel director each walked every part of the operation every day (and sometimes twice a day). Procedures, previously ignored, were updated and enforced, controls over the quality of recruits were installed and some minor engineering improvements were carried out. Excuses were banned ('Not interested in excuses – just learn from them and make sure you get it right next time' was the invariable reply), but reasons were listened to carefully.

Within six weeks output had reached the required level and within a further four weeks reached record levels, so much so that it had to be curtailed. Labour turnover dropped to manageable proportions and quality improved. The chairman was puzzled and asked the personnel director how so much had been achieved, when he had the feeling that so little had actually been done. The personnel director pointed out that the most valuable benefit had been simply talking to and, above all, listening to those at the sharp end, and providing them, by regular visits, with the confidence that senior management understood and would try to react to their concerns and deal with their problems. Such problems may have been correctly perceived as tiny within the scheme of operation – but they loomed large to those involved.

Key technique
In leading from the front, and sharing the problems and difficulties, the chairman had generated goodwill and motivated the workforce to do their best. The results were self-evident.

25

3

Starting to become a great communicator

'Taking aim'

Key learning points

1 Communicating requires a considerable and ongoing commitment
2 Until each party understands the other well, misinterpretations can arise
3 Responses can be conditioned by the circumstances
4 Simple slogans or themes are more effective than wordy policies.

As Henry V found, 'walking the job' is a very effective means of communicating with those at the sharp end and of motivating them. Not only does it have the benefit of allowing both sides an opportunity to understand the other, but also, and far more important, it can have a considerable benefit on the building of morale and enthusiasm, leading to improved commitment and increased output. Research (see Chapter 4) indicates that a majority of those with whom we must interface want to hear and learn more, and like nothing more than to see their leaders among them.

Case study 3.1
LESSONS FROM D-DAY – 1

It has already been mentioned how both George VI and Montgomery, in their different ways, recognised the need to encourage, motivate and sustain their followers. So keenly did the king feel this that (vigorously supported by Queen Elizabeth, now the Queen Mother) he wished to be present at the Normandy landings. Although unable to help in any material way, he felt that his presence would be a considerable benefit to the troops' morale. Plans were at quite an advanced stage for the king and queen to be aboard a ship just off the Normandy coast during the landings, when it was decided, in view of the danger to the monarch, as well as to the morale of the whole nation, that the idea should be dropped.

Key technique
It is said that fortune favours the brave and there is no doubt that seeing their king in their midst could, in 1944 in Normandy, have been as beneficial to the morale of the troops, as it was in 1415 a few miles away at Agincourt.

Walking the job and talking to the 'troops' is vitally beneficial, but it is also extremely time consuming and, when faced with pressing time demands, it is understandable if not excusable, if the opportunity of interfacing is passed up in favour of dealing with priority items on a manager's desk. However, motivating the workforce *is* the number one priority, as only through the actions of our workforce can we actually achieve the carefully laid plans we have devised. Obtaining input or reactions via third parties is valuable, though nowhere near as valuable as information gleaned from one's own first-hand experience.

27

Case study 3.2
LESSONS FROM D-DAY – 2

The planning and execution of the Allied invasion of Europe via the Normandy beaches, and the subsequent campaign which carried the Allies to Paris and Brussels within a few months, was a masterpiece of involved and detailed planning. The analysis, research, logistics etc. for such an undertaking required an immense amount of time. As the commander of land forces, Montgomery carried the responsibility for a great deal of this work and yet, from the day he was appointed to the task, he saw his prime task as the raising of the morale of the men who would do the fighting. Between January and May 1944, Montgomery visited every unit of the British and Canadian troops who would land on the Juno, Sword and Gold beaches, often speaking to thousands of men in a day. Not only did this give the ordinary soldier a chance to see and hear their commander, it also gave Montgomery an opportunity to put across to the men his concern to try and minimise the loss of life. 'What are your most valuable assets?' he would ask his men. 'Our guns?' they might reply. 'No they're not – your lives are our most important assets and I'm going to save them for you – now listen to me ...'.

Key technique
Focusing the attention on the matter closest to the soldiers' hearts, the fear of being killed or injured, was one way of ensuring attention. Being seen and being at the forefront of the action (all Monty's headquarters tended to be at or near the front line, while he would never wear a helmet but was always seen in his famous beret) demonstrated that he would back up with his own actions what he had put into words. With the immense demands on his time, it was a classic example that the real test of commitment to and communication with those who follow is not time but willpower. If we believe in something strongly enough we can and always will find the time. If we wish to be a great communicator, our own commitment is the first essential.

28

One of the favourite phrases of the chairman featured in case study 2.4 was 'the best manure is the farmer's boot', that is the best incentive is personal attention. It can also have unexpected benefits.

Case study 3.3
SPEAKING OUT SAVES COSTS

The managing director not only insisted that all employees should speak out but also, as part of his commitment to involving all employees directly, regularly 'walked the job' visiting most depots throughout the UK during the year. During a chat with a new clerk at the depot furthest from head office to ask if there was anything she did not understand, she replied that she could not understand why each week when her wages sheets were returned by the wages office they bore two additional names which had been both written in and then crossed out. It may have been beyond the comprehension of the young clerk, but the managing director immediately suspected what was eventually proved, that there was an extensive fraud being perpetrated by the wages department.

Key technique
Despite all the reports and controls, management may never really know what is going on without first-hand experience.

The multi-dimension response

Without regular and first-hand interfacing, one obtains a shallow and even misleading impression of reactions. After all it is perfectly possible for an individual to have at least six different versions of their viewpoint on the same viewpoint.

Case study 3.4
JOE'S DEVIOUS MIND

Joe was under pressure to achieve the dispatch of a set number of budgeted orders but was unable to move towards the target as the sales department was not releasing the orders. During his walking the job, Number 1 (i.e. the chief executive) saw Joe and asked him how things were – 'Yes sir, everything's fine'. Joe used these words since he felt that was the answer that Number 1 wanted to hear and he didn't want to let the side down. Number 1 had not realised, as had Henry V, that, without disguise, he would gain such a conditioned response.

Joe then met his immediate boss who also asked him how things were going. 'Oh, it's OK I suppose' Joe sighed with resignation, 'we've just got the usual trouble with sales department'. His response here is conditioned by the fact that if he complains too much, he might make waves, one of which might rebound to his disadvantage.

In the supervisors' rest room he complained more strongly to his opposite number in the sales department – 'That's the fifth time this week you've let me down – I need those orders now'. Making waves with colleagues may be less fraught with danger so the complaint can be more pointed. He stressed the previous poor record to try to act as an incentive and overstated the urgency of reaction for effect.

To his own team and subordinates he is even more pointed – 'We're not going to get those orders from those lazy so-and-so's in sales until tomorrow, so start work on XYZ instead'. The gloves being off, he felt he could be as critical as he liked, as he was among friends who probably shared his frustration and annoyance at the common enemy. Indeed, talking in this way, while it may undermine the prestige of the other department, can bind his own team more tightly.

At home he can unwind with his wife and tell her his true feelings – 'If I have another day like today, I'm jacking it in'. Somewhat obviously he may be unwilling to make such a comment in the workplace. If he says it to his manager, the latter might take it literally, while if he says it to his subordinates, it could demotivate them and make his task even more difficult.

Finally, before he drops off to sleep at the end of a harassing day he may even have a further version in his own mind – and who knows what that might be!

Number 1, assured in answer to his question, that 'everything's fine', may be somewhat disconcerted the following week to find a resignation from the employee who, the following day, did have another day 'like today'. This will be, at least in part, his own responsibility for hearing but not listening. Although walking the job is an essential part of an active communication process, it requires far more than a swift trot round the works. It is essential that genuine listening is part of the process. This cannot be achieved in a five second – 'Everything OK, Joe?', 'Yes sir – fine' exchange, although if even this brief exchange is repeated often enough tone alone may be sufficient to give the enquirer more insight into the other's true feelings. This apart, the longer the conversation and the more incisive the questions, inevitably the more likely the astute listener is to get nearer to the true views of the other party. This involves 'hearing' what is not said as much as what is said.

Unless the true views of the parties are discovered and listened to, there is little point in encompassing the principles and practice of communication, since the purpose is to improve matters in the widest sense. If managers are not prepared to invest time in listening to their staff (and vice versa) then nothing will be improved, since any decisions made will be based on an imperfect assessment and knowledge of the views and problems. As previously stated, the whole process is very time-consuming. The benefits in terms of greater awareness of aims and priorities, productivity and commitment are considerable, so it is hardly surprising that the investment can be costly.

Generating a commitment

Generating commitment of a workforce (that is making it care) requires the moulding of the aims and aspirations of employees, who may come from widely different backgrounds with a range of skills and array of perceptions and preferences, so that these meet the requirements of the employing organisation. Montgomery's aims were the defeat of the Nazi forces in France – aims that could be easily understood by his men. However, he captured their commitment by referring to their lives as the most important asset and ways of saving them as a means of applying their motivation to the job in hand.

In the commercial environment, setting aims poses two challenges:

- firstly, the aims of the organisation need to be codified and then constantly promulgated in language capable of immediate comprehension by the target audience; and

- secondly, the means by which the differing interests of employees can be guided to satisfy those aims must be laid down. Thus, employees must be communicated with, managed and led in previously agreed directions, and they must be sufficiently motivated to be prepared to sublimate personal aspirations.

Codifying the aims

It may seem to be stating the obvious to infer that all organisations have aims, as obviously they must have an aim or they would not exist. However, the true aims of organisations may not be those which are immediately apparent. Thus, profit-earning organisations may feel that since their purpose is to make a profit they need no further aims. A moment's thought will indicate that this cannot be the case, as there are many ways in which their profit could be obtained – not all of them legal. Presumably they are not willing to embrace all of the methods, including the illegal, by which profit can be made, in which case we need to delineate our philosophy, ethics or codes of conduct. We need to ask of our organisations questions such as those set out below.

31

Aim-creating questions

- Will the business seek to maximise profits at the expense of customer satisfaction, reputation and quality, or will it endeavour to provide good value for money, presenting its products at a reasonable time, in a reasonable state and endeavouring to build a reputation so that it obtains new business, and/or repeat business, by the recommendation of previous satisfied customers?

- Will it be a 'hire and fire' organisation – investing next to nothing in its employees and content to run with a high labour turnover, or will it wish to encourage long-term commitment by involving and training employees, thus engendering long-term employee stability?

and so on.

The need for clear 'aims-comprehension'

Sir John Harvey Jones, the former Number 1 of ICI, one of the UK's largest companies, in his book *Making it Happen* (Collins 1988) states 'with the best will in the world and the best board in the world, and the best strategic direction in the world, nothing will happen unless everyone down the line understands what they are trying to achieve and gives of their best'. The Industrial Society, which for over 70 years has promulgated the concept of employee communication and involvement as a positive force working towards the improvement of organisations' efficiency and productivity, runs courses on the need for, and devising of, company aims and vision. These courses, echoing Sir John's words, outline the benefits and disbenefits of adopting and communicating a common purpose as set out below.

Benefits accruing as a result of devising aims (and disbenefits resulting from their omission)

Gains:

- satisfied customers;
- maximum use of resources;
- committed and involved workforce;
- outward looking entity;
- entrepreneurial attitude;
- seizing market opportunities;
- capitalising on human assets.

Losses:

- lack of direction;
- wasted money and resources;
- insufficient use of resources;
- duplication of effort;
- demoralised staff;
- loss of customers;
- resistance to change.

So what should we include?

Alternative versions of company aims

Company A

■ We aim to provide our customers with the best quality products and services in order to be their preferred supplier, and to grow the business to utilise our total site capacity.

■ We are committed to the development and strengthening of partnerships with our external and internal customers and suppliers.

■ We will achieve this by the involvement and development of all employees to their potential and, by the commitment of all of us, working together for continuous improvement.

Company B

■ To provide a high standard of product and service to our customers at fair prices.

■ To provide our employees with the security of working for a successful company with job satisfaction, good remuneration and good working conditions, acknowledging their right to be informed and consulted on all matters which affect their work.

■ To earn sufficient money after tax to provide an adequate return on the savings that our shareholders have entrusted to our care, after reinvesting enough capital in the business to maintain the value of their assets and to ensure the healthy, long-term growth of the company.

■ To conduct our business with due care for the environment, and for the interests of the consumer and the general public.

Company C

■ To increase profit and productivity for the mutual benefit of customers, employees and shareholders.

■ To give complete customer satisfaction and have a proper responsibility for the community.

■ To provide opportunities for each employee to develop his or her capabilities.

■ To foster better communication between management and employees.

■ To develop better understanding, assist decision taking and encourage accountability.

■ To recognise the individual importance of every employee.

33

The three versions have great similarities. Each organisation has set out their commitment as a criteria against which all further actions can be measured, and against which the actions and progress of the business and its employees can be assessed. In addition, everyone involved should know their purpose – at what they are aiming. In 1992 the International Institute of Management of Geneva urged all organisations to establish their aims, and an increasing number of businesses have adopted and now use this idea. Further, some not only set out their aims, but also regularly measure progress against them and report how near they came to achieving them. Instituting this type of audit can help the business ensure it attains a consistent level of efficiency, as well as being a constant reminder to employees both of the aims and of the need to work towards their accomplishment.

Implementing the policy

34

If we are to lead we must communicate. If we are to motivate we must communicate. In a time when writing was practised only by a few, and even fewer could read, Henry V would have set little store by writing, arguing that the strength, flexibility and effectiveness of his tongue and body language was infinitely more effective than any piece of paper. Despite the technological advances made in the means of communication since 1415, it is arguable that little has changed from the muddy fields of Northern France in terms of the best way of expressing a leader's thoughts. True we have mass communication via our daily press, but even though a newspaper can take our thoughts to the furthermost parts of the globe within minutes, the recipient is still trapped by written language and only if they understand every word in exactly the way the writer intended will the message be received in the intent with which it was sent. Further, it will still lack emphasis and body language. It should not be overlooked that in the UK one in seven school leavers have difficulty reading and since, almost inevitably, some will be represented in our workforces we cannot assume that if we write something, it can be read by all, let alone understood.

Television can overcome both reading problems, and the lack of emphasis and body language, by carrying an image of the leader as they deliver their messages. However, without fully interactive recipient sets, each one linked so that each can hear what every other recipient has said, it still lacks the effect of a mass presentation.

Case study 3.5
CAR WARS

Vehicle manufacturer BMW uses television (via satellite transmission) to inform their staff in over 140 dealerships of the latest information regarding sales, marketing, data on competitors and so on. Since the programmes are developed weekly and edited overnight, the immediacy of the news is considerable. However, the company realised that while valuable, the messages were only flowing one way and refined the system so that staff were able to phone up during 'live' sessions and ask questions of executives 'on screen'.

Key technique
Getting the information to the recipient is a problem, but one which is usually solvable with determination and ingenuity, even if the time parameters are tight. The real test is trying to turn a single track information process into a dual response process – thereby converting information into communication.

35

Policy

A communication policy simply sets out the how and when, as well as the means that will be employed to communicate, as the example below demonstrates.

DRAFT COMMUNICATION POLICY

The company wishes to involve all personnel in its activities, to encourage their active participation in its progress including decision making, and to benefit by their comments and ideas. It commits itself to the regular dissemination of company information, and to the encouragement of inter-company and interpersonal communication which is to encompass personal as well as company activities. At all times the company will seek to keep all employees informed on plans and results, and on the effect on each part of the business. Regular briefing sessions will be conducted with all employees by representatives of senior management, and employees will be encouraged to express their views and concerns, as well as any suggestions at such briefing sessions.

1 Appointment

On appointment each employee will be given a wallet containing

(a) contract of employment

(b) employee handbook

(c) training, equal opportunities, health, safety and fire precautions statements

(d) copy of latest employee report

(e) copy of latest newsletter

(f) copy of any divisional/site publication

2 During employment employees will receive

(a) Annual/employee report (annually)

(b) Interim results (annually)

(c) Newsletter (quarterly/monthly/two weekly etc.)

(d) Local divisional newsletter or equivalent

(e) Regular management-organised briefing sessions

(f) Ad hoc briefing sessions as required

(g) Representation at works council/joint consultative meetings

(h) Copies of council/committee minutes

(i) Representation on safety/other committees

(j) Copies of safety/other committee minutes

3 Generally

Management are expected and encouraged to keep their employees informed of all activities and developments in an informal manner, there being no substitute for such face-to-face communication.

Senior management, via regular briefing and communication sessions, will attempt to keep employees up to date with all developments, and to listen to and attempt to deal with all concerns, suggestions and comments.

For their part employees are encouraged to take a lively interest in the activities of the company and, should there be anything on which they have insufficient information or where they are unsure, should be encouraged to ask their immediate superior immediately, or senior management at a briefing session. Should they not receive an adequate answer, they are entitled to pursue their query through the grievance procedure set out in the company handbook.

Senior management will also interface with employees on an ad hoc basis by means of regular 'walking the job' visits which, as far as possible, will be conducted on a truly informal and open basis.

Feedback (by both formal and informal means) will be sought from all employees on aspects of this policy.

Encapsulating the aim

Without wishing to belittle such a policy, since it is an outward sign of a commitment, the communication policy in this form is intended only as a reference document or a criteria. It is vitally important, but cannot be for everyday use. What is required is something which summarises the attitude of the company in a format capable of grabbing the attention and even of firing the imagination of those to whom it applies. What we want is the equivalent of Churchill's 'V-sign'. Under both guises – whether meant as a V for Victory symbol, captured in sound by the opening bars of Beethoven's Fifth Symphony which echo the letter 'V' in Morse code (Dit, dit, dit, dah), or as the somewhat coarse original version derived from the English longbowmen at Agincourt – the sign identified with the man and the struggle. Churchill's V-sign became an easily communicated and communicative symbol to all, both in the UK and on the occupied continent, of the British nation's will to resist despite the odds, and to overcome. So effective was it as both motivating force and stiffener of resistance that the enemy banned its use and promulgation under pain of death. V for Victory was a summation of the UK's policy of resistance to the aggressor.

37

Case study 3.6
IT'S A PLEASURE

On his appointment the new chairman wanted to enthuse and motivate the organisation. It was a company with traditional values and attitudes, and attempted to conduct its business and all relationships with a degree of respect for the views and interests of the other side. It could perhaps sum up its views as being assertive without being aggressive. The chairman coined the phrase 'It's a pleasure' and in his first message to the employees, exhorted them to try to adopt this phrase and all it stood for in their dealings, no matter whether these were with suppliers, customers or even internally.

The phrase caught on, with the retail side of the business even using it as a response to their customers. In three words the chairman had caught his philosophy of the whole group, and focused attention of all employees on a concept that was easy to understand and to employ. Whenever there was a dispute, aggravation could often be removed or put into a more appropriate perspective by an onlooker enquiring whether what had sparked the argument reflected the spirit of it 'being a pleasure'.

Key technique
The value of such a phrase is that it is instantly memorable, while the spirit, as well as the meaning, becomes a criteria in its own right.

This type of slogan is easy to project, to understand and to relate to. Every aspect of constructive communication can be tied into it – management or cascade briefings should be pleasurable in terms of involving employees and hearing their views; written information should be pleasurable in terms of ensuring a clear promulgation of adequate and timely facts; the dissemination of information and taking part in communication should be pleasurable as an aid to greater awareness of the requirements of the organisation for mutual benefit, and so on. The implementation of all that such a phrase stands for should ensure a mutual respect and willingness to commit to the aims of the organisation from the majority of those involved.

Case study 3.7
POSTSCRIPT

In 1964 a schoolteacher in Essex was asked by her class what the 'D' in 'D-Day' stood for. Since she was unsure, she wrote to Churchill who was by then nearing the end of his life. To her considerable surprise she received a personal letter from the man himself, virtually by return, explaining that the letter simply stood for the day on which the invasion would take place.

Key technique
A mark of true leadership and a great communicator is an attention to detail. Insignificant though the item may be to the leader who has the advantage of the holistic view of the whole endeavour, to the person at the sharp end the item may have far greater significance, while the fact that the leader found time to answer it is a very effective way of creating rapport and commitment.

Breaking down barriers

'Logistics, statistics and supplies'

Key learning points

1 **Without management commitment, communication cannot exist**
2 **Management must be provided with communication skills**
3 **Personal and departmental relationships need to be clear**
4 **Engendering pride by means of inspiration and enthusiasm can unleash positive commitment.**

The Advisory, Conciliation and Arbitration Service (ACAS) has for over 20 years been involved in the process of trying to improve relationships in the workplace. In 1994 ACAS published a guide 'Employee communications and consultation', noting as it did so that during the 1980s and 1990s it had seen an increasing emphasis on regarding employees as 'human resources', whose abilities could be improved (even exploited) in order to increase productivity. According to ACAS 'good' employee communication has a 'measurable effect on organisational success' through improved management decision making, greater trust and increased job satisfaction. The report clearly differentiates between employee communications and involvement, defining the former as 'the provision and exchange of information and instructions which enable an organisation to function efficiently'. The operative word in this case is 'efficiently', while the definition includes the word 'exchange' which echoes the distinction between the provision of information and the 'two-way' nature of communication highlighted in Figure 2.1. Having stated that communication is an integral part of every manager's job, the report goes on to suggest ways in which the process can be effected.

Recommendations re communication from ACAS report 'Employee communications and consultation'

- a clear statement of policy should be drawn up;

- those responsible at each level should be identified;

- the means by which communication is promulgated and encouraged should be established;

- those responsible for the communication process, as well as those with whom the organisation wishes to communicate should be trained; and

- the whole system should be monitored regularly.

The missing link

It is often the case that Number 1 (and indeed the whole board) can be completely committed to the principle and practice of employee communication, yet the situation does not improve. This is rarely the fault of employees as most would be only too glad to have their efforts and concerns recognised – even if the recognition involves criticism rather than praise. 'Praise me, scold me – just never ignore me' is a phrase which few employees may have heard. Most, however, would subscribe to its philosophy. People want to be noticed, to be appreciated, to be treated as mature individuals. People manage their lives, their families and their children, and have to take decisions, some very difficult. It is patronising in the extreme to treat them as if they were fools or children – indeed it is not only patronising, it is dangerous, as it invites resentment. In our employees we have a captive audience, and one that is only too prepared to listen and to comment, and to accept their responsibility for the communication process. Failure to take advantage of such a receptive audience can only damage the morale and commitment of those on whom the organisation depends for its output and continuation.

Research across a cross-section of organisations indicates that people have preferences in communication means. The prime preference is face-to-face and personal communication. The notice on the notice board may be a means of effective information, but one cannot ask questions of a piece of paper. Face-to-face communication provides that opportunity. Next in order of preference come small briefings conducted by local management or supervision, followed by large briefings conducted by senior management. Last in this order of preference comes printed material – mainly for the point already made, but also, since no matter how much it is designed to entice readership, it is essentially lifeless, lacking the spontaneity of the informal (or even, formal) briefing, lacking the emphasis of body language, and, above all, lacking the binding, motivating and incentivising effect of a personal presentation.

Communication – the hidden demand

MORI, the market research and survey organisation, constantly monitors employee responses to company initiatives. In a 1994 analysis they discovered that employees' satisfaction with the amount of communication they received from their employers had hardly changed in 20 years – although it must be said that expectations have probably risen during that period. In response to the question – 'Do you receive sufficient communication?' only 49 per cent felt that they did. However, 97 per cent of the employees interviewed felt that it was important that their company communicated with them. One conclusion that we can draw from this research is that once we try to communicate with employees we will be pushing against an open door. In terms of involvement other MORI research indicated that two-thirds of the workforce are prepared to get involved, nearly half want to be more involved than they are, whilst only 3 per cent feel that communication is unimportant. With this kind of anticipated response, it is difficult to envisage that Number One will have any problems gaining the attention of the employees – providing the right conduit is used.

Knowledge is power

Unfortunately it seems that many managers, perhaps those promoted to, or even beyond the level of competence (the so-called 'Peter principle'), resist passing on information to their workforce and hoard information believing that if it is recognised that they have information to which others are not privy, this increases their prestige. Ignoring the fact that to some extent this questions the maturity and ability of the incumbent to manage themselves, let alone other people, the ACAS guidelines acknowledge this by suggesting that those responsible for the communication process should be identified.

Case study 4.1
HOARDING

The company, after a period in which there was absolutely no communication, was painfully working through an era where open management was being encouraged. As part of the process, a staff newspaper was launched, with the invitation that employees should contribute items for inclusion. An assurance was given that, other than anonymous or offensive items, all items would be published. However, there seemed little response from many areas of the business. The executive responsible was constantly walking the job and, intrigued by this, questioned various managers and manageresses on the response of their staff to the newspaper. He found that in some locations, although sufficient copies had been sent for each employee, these had not been distributed at all, while in others, the employees' own copies were only given to them during breaks and were collected afterwards!

Key techniques

1 You cannot afford to assume that your own instinctive reaction when posed with such a requirement will be shared by all, particularly where there has been a conditioning of response over a number of years. Thereafter, each time the newspaper was sent out there was a covering note to the person in charge at each site, requesting that individual copies be given out within 24 hours of receipt, and stressing there was no objection (indeed there was a positive invitation) to employees removing their own copies from the premises and showing their families.

2 Distribution of information, particularly that which is designed to generate feedback, needs to be carefully considered. Too often, despite the message being given every attention, its actual promulgation is a last-minute, hastily arranged affair. The effect is that the whole purpose is negated by what should be a routine administration exercise. Dates of publication, means of conveyance, collection places, timing, all need to be notified in advance to those responsible. Ideally information should be received by all the target audience simultaneously – this is unlikely to be achieved if the actual logistics are left to the last moment or given insufficient attention.

43

While case study 4.1 has its humorous side, underlying it is the serious problem of ensuring that whenever information is to be promulgated in order to prompt response and involvement it does not become blocked by the intervening layers of management.

Sieving

Blocking information can be relatively easily overcome once it is known, which is the reason for suggesting that the whole system is regularly checked. In checking reactions and feedback it will very quickly become apparent if the flow is impeded. Action then needs to be taken to remove the impediment. A greater problem can be that of 'sieving' information. Like the famous military command 'Send reinforcements we're going to advance' which, having passed through four or five relays of command, was eventually received as 'Send three and fourpence we're going to a dance', messages can become distorted the more they have to be relayed. Using the cascade system of briefing, the enthusiasm and invigorating effect of Number 1's rousing 'call to arms' can be progressively watered down.

44

Case study 4.2
THAT'S NOT WHAT I MEANT

Number 1 felt that the organisation needed a boost to its morale and addressed all the senior managers stressing the fact that there were new orders to be won, which would ensure the factories worked to capacity for at least a year. One of the aims of the address was to reassure everyone that there was no question of short time working or losing employees through redundancy. The request was to pass the message on 'right through the whole company'.

The senior managers went away, and saw the middle and junior managers. The message they heard was 'We've got an awful lot to do in the next year, so get everyone cracking on it'.

In turn the junior managers saw their supervisors and passed them the message that 'We really need to crack down on everything for the next 12 months'.

The supervisors, some of whom were having discipline problems, saw this as an opportunity and told their employees 'Unless you lot pull your fingers out and improve productivity you'll all be out of jobs by the end of the year'.

The trade union representatives were extremely concerned that redundancies might be in the offing and immediately requested a meeting with the factory manager at which they threatened a work-to-rule unless the full facts were put before them.

Key technique
This is the inherent danger of cascade briefing (see Chapter 6). If Number 1 cannot speak personally and widely then a message must be consigned to paper and distributed. Even then the words used should be examined carefully for unwanted undertones or misinterpretations. Simple language needs to be used; any use of jargon or words not in everyday use can confuse and mar the effectiveness of the message.

Unblocking the pipe

Managers who are perceived to be communication blocks or 'sieves' need to have the point and benefits of the required 'flow' carefully explained to them. Employee communication must be promoted simply as an additional tool which will help them achieve their aims. If an appraisal system is in force (see Chapter 11), those interviews provide opportunities of ensuring that managers understand and comply with both principles and practice of active communication. Research from the USA indicates that 94 per cent of people have no great interest in being awkward or difficult, and only want to do their job and 'get on with things'. This leaves only 6 per cent who are 'awkward customers' requiring special handling. Some of these will undoubtedly have risen to the position of management and such interviews may not be easy. Ultimately the point needs to be made that in the 'active communication organisation' people are unlikely to be well regarded or to proceed further unless they are seen to have positively embraced the concept and practice. But convincing managers of the benefits should be a better way of 'selling' the concept, than wielding the big stick. Company rescue specialist, Sir Lewis Robertson, stated at a British Association of Industrial Editors conference 'successful organisations take communications seriously. They succeed by stimulating and supporting a regular flow of sound, reliable information to all proper audiences. This requires conscious, active effort and sustained attention at senior level'.

45

Management skills required to communicate effectively

- Tenacity – to find out or help to work out what is to be communicated.
- Sensitivity – to appreciate the different needs of different audiences.

- Skill to formulate clearly and simply, in language and style adapted to the audience, a crystallised statement of the message.

- Honesty, respect and clarity are also needed (while conversely condescension, complication and a patronising style must be avoided), and are achieved by serious thought and sensitive awareness of the audience's interests.

Source: Sir Lewis Robertson, chairman, Stakis PLC

To the recalcitrant manager, perhaps setting out the skills required and querying whether he or she has them, may provide sufficient challenge to overcome any reluctance.

The open door

Not, as previously mentioned, that managers will encounter much resistance as they grapple with the challenge. Most employees are only too willing to listen.

Analysis of employee views of information/communication processes

- Ninety-five per cent of employees state that they do not wish to receive information via the grapevine, although almost 50 per cent state that that is how they do receive it.

- Sixty-eight per cent of employees felt that there is not enough opportunity to inform their employing organisation about things that affect their work. (Since some of these must concern problems that mitigate against the effectiveness of their work, the potential improvement in productivity is considerable.)

- Fifty-nine per cent of employees feel inhibited about speaking out. They feel such action could damage their future and/or career prospects.

- Fifty-eight per cent of employees feel that the training they receive is ineffective.

- Fifty-six per cent of employees do not feel that their employing organisations appreciate their efforts.

- Over 50 per cent would like meetings to be part of the communication process.

Source: MORI

Further research by MORI in 1994 found that generally employees' loyalty to their organisations was reducing and the credibility of senior management to employees was falling. Against the background of the research by MORI and McKinsey, it is difficult to overstress the urgent need to improve matters for the benefit of all involved. Indeed, concern at this trend has been one of the contributory factors behind the launch of the Employee Communications Association. Sponsored jointly by British Telecom, Parcelforce and the Industrial Society, the association seeks to 'professionalise' the role of those working to improve employee communications, and to provide them with skills and confidence to tackle the challenges.

'But where do I fit in?'

Although to top management the structure and organisation of the entity, and the interrelationship of constituent parts may be well defined and clear, to those below this level, even including middle and junior management let alone employees at the sharp end, these relationships may seem difficult to comprehend or appreciate. While job descriptions and appraisals (see Chapter 11) may define the individual's exact duties, their role in the great scheme of things may be difficult to understand. Before Agincourt, Henry V explained his strategy to his archers, made them build a defensive fence of stakes, behind which they sheltered, in the shape of a funnel into which eventually the French army was forced and slaughtered as it found less and less space in which it could manoeuvre. The various parts of Henry's compact force knew what each was doing and successfully sprang the trap. Had each part of the force not understood the role of the other, that cohesion of effort, which was such an important part of the victory, could not have been achieved.

47

Case study 4.3
FALSE ECONOMY

The quality control department of an electrical household goods manufacturer was concerned to improve the 'swift delivery' reputation of the organisation and invested in a computer software package which was able to plot the swiftest route for the delivery vans. To try to further improve deliveries the delivery time allowed at each address was cut. What the planners had not realised was (a) the drivers knew their delivery 'patch' and short cuts, etc., and trying to follow the computer-produced route took more time (instead of using the maps in their heads they had to use those produced by the computer), and (b) not all householders were either in, or answered the door swiftly, or were able instantly to tell the delivery driver and his mate where to locate the new item. In a period of four weeks two vans were involved in accidents, trying to make up time, while their loads were written off.

Key technique
Where changes are required there is an increased need for two-way communication between all involved. The MORI research found that change tends to reduce the rating (that is effectiveness) of communications. The full implications of all changes need to be thought through and the concerns of all involved must be addressed positively rather than being dismissed or overlooked.

48

Case study 4.4
'I DIDN'T THINK IT MATTERED'

At the end of the process the machinist was supposed to put the piece of metal she had produced through a polisher which, apart from polishing the metal, also removed any remaining imperfections. However, she had not been told that the 'polisher' also 'smoothed' and, when under pressure, sometimes passed through the output without 'polishing' it. Very quickly the next department in the process began to receive complaints of failure, which generated a major investigation. The fault was eventually traced to the fact that the metal parts had not been finally 'smoothed' and the operator's short cut was discovered.

Key technique
The relationships of departments and the use to which the end product is put need to be explained to ensure appreciation of 'why' certain actions must be taken. Withholding explanation or not fully explaining the relationships can prove costly.

Making relationships clear

Organisation and work flow charts should be utilised to ensure that all departments understand both their role and their relationship with other interlocking departments. In the two examples (Figures 4.1 and 4.2), the same structure has been depicted.

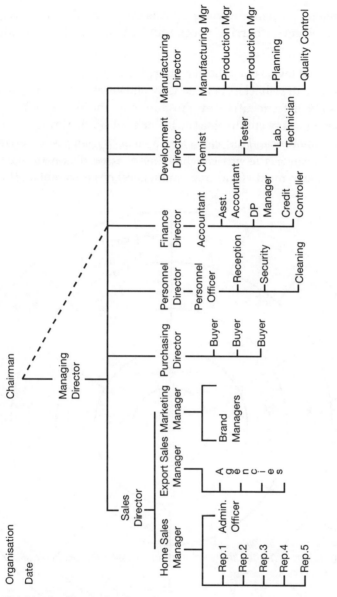

Figure 4.1 Vertical organisation chart

The more levels between top management and the sharp end, the greater the problem of communication. As Sir John Harvey Jones commented 'You have to destroy the hierarchy if you possibly can. I am a great believer in chaos and considerable tolerance of difference, because I believe the key to organisation is speed. Practically every system we put in business is to stop people doing things'.

Unfortunately, in communication terms every 'level' must be regarded as either a potential 'barrier' to communication or a 'sieve' to reduce its content.

The 'vertical levels of authority' chart is in very common use but suffers from two drawbacks. It is usually shown as a pyramid, with the chairperson/chief executive at the 'top' and the foot soldiers at the 'bottom', which may emphasise the latter's subservient role – a possibly unwanted inference. This can be overcome by simply inverting the pyramid. However, the vertical chart has another disadvantage in that it implies departments (and their managers) or personnel on the same

50

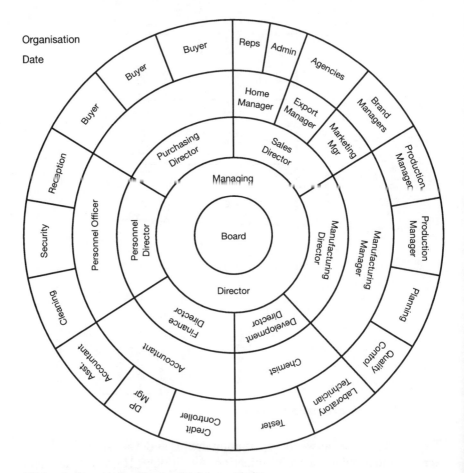

NB Levels are not indicative of authority or seniority.

Figure 4.2 Circular organisation chart (from the author's *ONE STOP Personnel Management* (ICSA Publishing 1992))

level have the same 'importance' or 'value'. Either the relative positions of departments and/or personnel should be carefully checked and discrepancies eradicated, or the chart should carry a note such as 'The positioning of departments on certain levels is not indicative of importance, status or responsibility'. Even with such a warning it is difficult to overcome the strong inference of 'equality' (or 'inequality') presented by the visual image. First impressions (in this case the visual image) are very important and lasting.

As an alternative, the chart can be drawn with departments depicted within circular bands emanating from the board, which is shown as the core. This overcomes the 'top' and 'bottom' overtones, and blurs the problem that may arise over levels of importance and/or authority. However, it also blurs the chain of command which may be a drawback.

Departmental relationships

Case study 4.5
I KNOW WHAT I DO – BUT WHAT DO YOU DO?

In 1990 Daventry District Council underwent a major structural change. Subsequently, partly as a result of a staff survey (see Chapter 14) the council identified internal communication as a major factor which would assist in dealing with the organisational change. However, what also emerged from the staff survey was that while most employees liked and understood what their own department did, they did not really know what happened in other departments.

Key technique
Ignorance of what the other person does may mean problems go unsolved, disputes over responsibility proliferate and demarcation arguments destroy effective performance.

Figure 4.3 is a chart indicating the working relationships of a department forming part of a productive process, drawing raw materials and part-finished product, applying its own work and passing it on to the next department in the process. The 'process' position is established and, if linked to departmental aims and levels of performance, at least the essential working relationships are clarified.

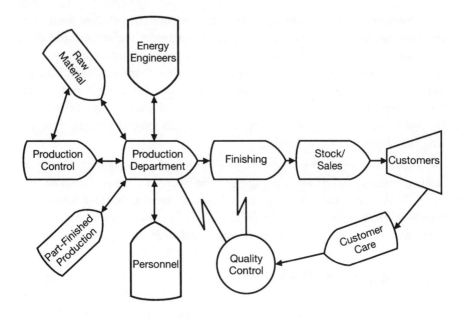

Figure 4.3 Working relationships

The other teams

One effect of the publication of organisation charts is to try to under-line the necessity for individuals to think of themselves as members of a team. The creation of a team and of team spirit tends to result in the situation where the whole is greater than the sum of the parts. While I have used several examples from the military experience to demon-strate leadership in action, one could also draw from the field of sport, where the most successful clubs tend to be those which create the best team spirit. To achieve this they need good captains, whose greatest task is to motivate. As Trevor Bailey, one of England's best test cricket players said, 'Good captains [leaders] tend to make good players [employees] rise above themselves'.

In football, not only is there usually a captain on the field endeav-ouring to motivate the other players to give of their best, but also on the touchline, often yelling instructions and guidance, are both a manager and a coach. Those who know little about the game might be forgiven for querying whether two or three people giving possibly conflicting views simultaneously might be counter-productive. However, it is often said that the onlooker sees more of the game, so it is possible that the extra dimension of touchline perception can help guide and motivate the players. It is certainly true that teams often rise above themselves when their supporters are roaring them on. Praise and encouragement are powerful motivators, and are most effective when contributed in person rather than in writing or some other impersonal format.

Creating a better team spirit

- Acknowledge achievement – praise is an extremely effective means of motivation and it costs nothing!

- Monitor and demonstrate progress – praising progress and, when there is no progress, the need for effort is obvious

- Share the preferred tasks – and the awkward tasks, so that all members of the team take their turn at both.

- Ensure the leader does his or her fair share of the awkward tasks – example is a powerful motivator

- Encourage team members to discuss their concerns and problems.

- Encourage everyone to look for opportunities in problems to think positively.

53

As St Benedict said as long ago as the sixth century 'those in authority are not to be above the group' – the leader *must* be part of the team.

PIEmaking

The aim of organisation charts, of communication, of generating a better team spirit is primarily the creation of an identity of the individual with the whole; a feeling which can only be generated when there is a feeling of mutual trust and understanding – a prime aim of the whole communication process. A by-product of identification with the whole, and of the creation of mutual trust and understanding, should be a simultaneous creation of a feeling of pride in the endeavour. This is valuable, since not only does it tend to generate real commitment to the organisation and its products, but also employees who are proud of what they and their organisation achieve are good ambassadors for their product or service. To generate pride, we need to create enthusiasm, and to generate enthusiasm, we need to inspire the workforce – as did Number 1 in case study 4.2. Had all the workforce heard the original speech and been able to query anything they did not understand, there can be little doubt that they would have been at least reassured and, if Number 1 was a good leader and communicator, they should have been encouraged and inspired to 'go for it'. The relationship between these three – pride, inspiration and enthusiasm – is all-important for the successful organisation and since one tends to generate the other they are best depicted as a never-ending circle. It is certainly true that nothing succeeds like success.

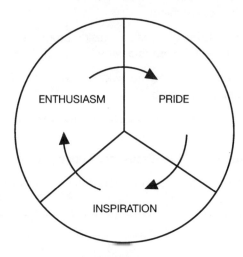

Figure 4.4 Baking a communication PIE

5

Defeating rumour

'Beware – there's a fifth column at work'

Key learning points

1 Only effective 'official' communication can undermine the power of the grapevine
2 Only if communication is consistent, continuous and reliable is it effective
3 Communication must be honest, reliable, free from hype and user-friendly
4 Successful communication (as well as pending legal moves) may lead to the requirement for a full involvement policy

The effect of good communication is the greater involvement of the employees harnessing effort to pre-set aims, and improving commitment, output and productivity for mutual benefit, or in other words creating the circle of pride, inspiration and enthusiasm shown in Figure 4.4. Hopefully the wordy items, such as 'aims', 'policy' and so on, can be encapsulated into an instantly recognisable catchphrase which can itself then be projected and promoted with enthusiasm and professionalism. The phrase needs to be treated as a brand name – the brand in this case being the philosophy of the organisation *vis-à-vis* its employees and others to whom it relates or with whom it interfaces.

Another benefit of the practical application of such a policy should be a reduction in the unease and concern that can be generated within the organisation by the operation of the informal grapevine or 'rumour machine'. No matter how extensive the research, one can rarely find the source of rumours, while no amount of denial and investigation seem able to stop their generation. The problem with rumours is that often they contain a germ of truth on which is spun a web of untruth, exaggeration and disinformation, all of which can work negatively against the motivation and confidence of employees. Trying to separate these twin aspects in order to confirm the truth, yet deny the falsehood, can prove very difficult and in any event is likely to be counter-productive.

> **Case study 5.1**
> **DENYING THE NON-EXISTENT**
>
> The newly appointed personnel director was attempting to improve communications and involvement generally, even though the company had a history of poor communication. She set up regular briefing meetings with both union representatives and representatives of non-unionised employees. Despite every effort, in the early days rumours tended to proliferate. At one meeting when she had categorically denied (totally truthfully) that redundancies were being considered (the latest rumour), it was suggested that a notice denying the rumour be posted. She refused, pointing out that it was difficult enough trying to ensure that there was communication concerning things that were to happen without confusing everyone by giving credence to things that were not going to happen.
>
> *Key technique*
> *The problem with such a suggestion is that it could put an idea into the heads of some of those who had not previously thought of it. It is usually more appropriate to adopt a policy of never commenting on rumour, thus seeking to denigrate by refusing to acknowledge. In this way the rumour-mongers are left 'punching cotton wool'.*

Rumour is often described as being multi-headed and, rather like the multi-headed Hydra of Greek mythology who grew two heads every time one was cut off, denial of one rumour can generate more, and even wilder, versions. Rumour's purpose is usually two faced, seeking to inform but only in a way in which mutual trust is undermined and unease is created. Consistent and reliable communication can play an important role in removing its credence, thereby discrediting it and negating its damage potential. Providing employer sourced information and communication is honest, consistent and reliable, it will often give the lie to such misinformation, destroying its appeal and credibility. It is unlikely that the rumour machine can ever be eliminated, but its effects can certainly be minimised. Certainly it can never be contained without commitment to a regular supply of genuine, timely and up-to-date information.

Case study 5.2
MOVING STORY

Situated in London, the company had recently recruited a new manager from a company that had moved to South Wales. At the same time, as part of its commitment to trying to market its products more aggressively, the company had changed its advertising agents to a larger partnership. To announce its success the agency advertised in the national press that the company 'had moved to Chetwynd Haddons'. Unfortunately the company had been through a bad patch, with inadequate communication and consequent mistrust, and the advertisement was taken as indicating that the whole company was moving to this new location which was 'somewhere in Wales'. The supporting 'evidence' was the appointment of the manager who, five years previously, had overseen such a move of one of the company's competitors!

Key technique
The coincidence of the agency's unusual name, the fact that it could pass for a Welsh name and the newly appointed manager having overseen a move to Wales was strange. But the rumour took life from the inadequate communication processes that were in force in the company. This is not a situation that can be eradicated in a swift denial, even with all proof supplied. True, that may scotch the current rumour, but only a consistent provision of adequate and reliable information will contain the rumour-monger.

The real problem of the rumour is that, human nature being what it is, we are usually more ready to believe bad news than good. Perhaps it would be worth employers displaying the 'cautionary tale' set out below.

A cautionary tale

- If something is interesting it is possibly wrong.
- If something is very interesting it is probably wrong.
- If something is extremely interesting, it is almost certainly wrong!

Rumours always tend to feature 'something extremely interesting', which is usually bad news and thus becomes, almost by definition,

believable, particularly as there may be a germ of truth buried somewhere. If the best productivity is achieved when people are feeling
secure and well motivated, we will never be able to generate the optimum when those responsible for output have items of concern to dis-
tract them from the job in hand.

58

> **Case study 5.3**
> **TAKING ONE'S EYE OFF THE BALL**
>
> During the six-month project to relocate employees into alternative jobs
> and to protect employment as far as possible, recounted in case study 2.2,
> there was one occasion when the consultant was not able to visit the fac-
> tory for just over two weeks. Despite him notifying the workforce that there
> would be a gap, but that it was nothing to worry about, during his absence,
> previous poor relationships and mistrust resurfaced. At the same time a
> deal to sell part of the operation with continuity of employment for around
> half the workforce was finally concluded.
>
> On his next visit, however, he found that not only were the workforce
> ignorant of this welcome news, but also rumours were circulating that the
> closure was being brought forward and passions were running so high
> that there was talk of an immediate walkout.
>
> The local management had done nothing to rectify either matter – simply
> leaving the consultant to sort out the problem, which he did by means of
> calling a mass meeting, telling them everything he knew and pointing out
> that although he could understand their concern, a walkout was certainly
> in no one's interests – least of all their own.
>
> *Key technique*
> *Honest communication is a regular requirement and, in times of con-*
> *cern or crisis, it is a regular necessity. Gaps can give totally the wrong*
> *impression.*

Using the grapevine

At any one time up to 20 per cent of the average workforce may have a
serious personal problem affecting their performance. Rumours are
based on work problems and thus their effect can be more widespread,
far more serious for those with their own personal problems and swift
to multiply. But it should not be overlooked that two can play at the
rumour game. Although potentially dangerous, knowing that there is a

grapevine can provide management with a means of achieving its own ends.

Case study 5.4
FIGHTING THE WRONG BATTLE

The company had developed the habit of spending considerable time in wage rate negotiations. In an effort to short-cut the process, a rumour was started deliberately, that the company was to offer only 3 per cent, at a time when 6 to 8 per cent increases tended to be the norm. So strong was the rumour that the union negotiators attended the first meeting with the perception that they had a real fight on their hands. When the management in response to the union demand of a 9 per cent increase, suggested 5 per cent provided agreement could be gained within three days, and pointed out that the negotiators could return to their members indicating that they had increased the 'management's' figure from 3 to 5 per cent, the deal was swiftly done.

Key technique
This kind of pre-emptive action may only work provided the other side can be shown to have had some input. Here the union negotiators had been able to justify their existence.

59

Activating the plan

The adoption of a communication/involvement policy encapsulated with a memorable phrase sets the total framework within which open and frank communication between employer and employee can be fostered. Inevitably many aspects of it relate to the dissemination of information via the written word. It is important, no matter how much we rely on this form of information, to remember that communication is unlikely to be achieved by the production of glossy company brochures, newspapers or reports. Indeed research suggests that the glossier that kind of publication, the less the rapport it may generate with many employees. Communicating is part and parcel of every activity undertaken in the attainment of the aims of the organisation, and the motivation of the employees to achieve those aims – thus all management style and practice must be related to the common aim. We need to communicate and involve employees in order to:

- explain requirements and agree action,
- guide progress and attainment,

- consider problems and agree solutions,
- review results and implement new actions,

and the key to success is the implementation and constant adherence of the programme. There are several factors which need to be addressed in adopting such a practice as set out below.

Communication dissemination – essential ingredients

- commitment;
- reliability;
- honesty;
- accuracy – that is avoiding hype;
- telling it like it is;
- user-friendliness.

Commitment

To ensure the success of the process it needs commitment from the top management right from the start and constantly thereafter. Unless top management provide a lead, and constantly refer and relate to the process, it simply cannot succeed. Experience indicates, however, that often it is not so much the lack of support from top management as from middle management that threatens to throttle the concept. Middle management may see the process as a threat to their position, and steps need to be taken to provide reassurance and to involve them in the process. They need to be encouraged to think of the concept as an additional management tool (which, if used well, it can be), rather than as a threat to their position (which, should they resist, it may be). The board needs to ensure that all those responsible for carrying it out are equally committed to its precepts and implementation. Almost inevitably there will be some, either through lack of faith in the benefits, or lack of time, or both, who will not adhere to these requirements. These reactions must be anticipated, answered and any residual misgivings eradicated or it will fail. Even if it fails in only one area, the shortcomings in that one area will tend to undermine the progress being made in other areas. Thus, it is essential that top management appreciate the damaging effect of this potential backlash. It may be necessary to provide training and coaching resources, while 'doubters' and those who feel unsure, may need to be prompted and supported to ensure they carry out their role in the manner required. The benefits of the scheme in terms of achieving improved output and commitment need to be stressed. In addition, managers need to be involved in implementing the scheme, in setting aims for their individual departments and employees.

Reliability

In announcing a commitment to such a process – indeed even constructing a policy statement – expectations will be raised. Unless these are satisfied then the situation could be worse than had no such commitment ever been made. Further, instituting a consistent communication process is a long-term project. It is not an instant remedy and there may not be instant results. Unless the process is both ongoing and reliable, there will be no credibility, without which it cannot survive. It is better to have a little communication regularly than a great deal spasmodically. Human beings are creatures of habit and we should seek to use this predeliction by creating habits for our own ends. Giving information regularly creates both habit and anticipation. Anticipation in turn creates a demand – a demand that must be satisfied.

61

Case study 5.5
IT MUST BE DISASTROUS

The managing director had to interface with his American superiors on a regular basis, and had adopted the habit of holding an informal briefing shortly after his return to update the employees on progress and developments. On one occasion, however, he was so behind with routine matters, as well as feeling ill, that the briefing was not held. Since he looked so grim the rumour swiftly evolved that bad news was imminent. He was horrified when he was told and quickly convened the usual meeting.

Key technique
If anticipated communication is missed, assumptions will be made. Regular briefings should never be cancelled even if it appears there is little to say. The cancellation, or non-convening, carries a semiotic message of its own.

Honesty

The process must be treated with complete trust and the content with complete honesty by the management, or it will have no credibility. Although commitment and morale, and almost inevitably, productivity, will be improved by starting a full communication process, this will be stultified unless, at all times, the process is consistent and the content is reliable. If, at any time, the company is not being honest and truthful, the integrity of the process will be damaged – possibly irreparably. This is not meant to imply that there may not be occasions when information must be restricted because of a need to respect the confidentiality of an individual or even part of the business. Employees are not fools and most will appreciate that for sound reasons, from time to time, employers will need to be less than candid. However, this maturity of approach can only be engendered by ensuring that, other than such exceptions, honesty and openness prevail and reliance is assured.

Case study 5.6
MOVING STORY (PART 2)

The company which did not even wish to move to Wales set up a number of projects aimed at improving information and communication. One of these was a joint consultative committee at which, 12 months after the 'move' rumour, the question of whether the company would ever move was posed. The director pointed out that the premises were over 90 years old, were situated in a congested area of London and, having been designed for a labour-intensive operation, were not ideal for the current mechanised process.

While a new building would be ideal, the cost would be considerable and the implementation timetable could be at least five years long. Since the matter had not even been considered seriously this indicated that such a possibility was at least five years away.

Key technique
Being as open as possible at all times should be the watchword and be understood generally to be the watchword.

Accuracy – avoiding 'hype'

'Hype', a widely used term, is short for 'hyperbole', defined in the dictionary as 'exaggerated statement not meant to be taken literally'. In view of that definition, it is fair to assert that such items should not form any part of employee communication. Sadly, however, there are too many examples of employee communication material which do contain an amount of hype that most employees will swiftly recognise for what it is. 'Hype' is often used as a 'selling tool', but employees do not need to be 'sold' the organisation, they know it too well, and to a certain extent they have already 'bought' it by agreeing and continuing to work for it. The inclusion of hyped items in material which is supposed to inform and communicate facts tends to destroy the credibility of the facts as well as the whole process, and may create an employee backlash.

The inclusion of 'hype' in such circumstances is patronising. Where present, the underlying message, easily recognisable by the employees, is that the author feels that the employees will 'swallow anything'. In other words they are thought to be so gullible that accuracy and truth can be ignored.

63

Telling it like it is

Employees are adults and deserve to be treated as such. They are the first to appreciate that the progress, or lack of progress, of their employer cannot always be a matter of good news. Being prepared to deal openly with bad news is an essential concomitant of a communication policy, and any failure to address the problems and difficulties that will be occasioned by such news will once again undermine the whole intent and value of the process. Employees know from personal experience that problems do occur and most are perfectly capable of dealing with such problems. It would be naïve for employees to expect all the operations and plans of their organisation to work in accordance with expectations, and few will have such expectations. Hence, providing the foundation of constant communication has been laid, the arrival or announcement of bad news should cause less of an hiatus than may be anticipated. Most employees are quite capable of handling bad news; they may not like it, but usually they can understand and accept it. What they cannot accept is either not being told at all or not being told the full truth. This is understandable, since once more the patronising implication is that they are not capable of being able to handle the news, which the great majority manifestly are. Obviously it helps if people have been given information as part of a continued process and are thus aware of the background when an announcement is made.

> **Case study 5.7**
> **IT'S OBVIOUS REALLY**
>
> In the mid 1980s the Maynards Group, Confectionery, Tobacco and News (CTN) retailing division, hit by a doubling of VAT on its products (which had to compete with zero-rated food products), rapidly increasing rents forced by the property boom, as well as by disproportionately increased rates and wage increases, found its profitability wiped out, despite considerable efforts to offset such effects. A process of communicating financial results had been started some years earlier and through regular user-friendly reports and country-wide briefings, such results were explained to the staff. Following two years' losses, the decision was taken to withdraw from CTN retailing and the staff were informed. Out of around 2,500 employees made redundant, only one was in any way abusive when the decision was announced. The reaction from the remainder was very much 'Well, we could see it coming, you couldn't go on losing money in this division – it was obvious to us'.
>
> *Key technique*
> *Senior management had regularly walked the job, communicated with and briefed the employees, and so all were well aware of the reality of the situation. Not only were senior managers well known to most of the full-time and many of the part-time staff, but a degree of trust and mutual understanding had been built up over the years. It was a source of considerable pride that in closing the shops or in preparing them for transfer to new owners, only a tiny proportion suffered stock losses which tend to be endemic in such a situation.*

64

User-friendliness

Before launching a new product, a producer normally carries out market research, and using its results refashions and redesigns the product until it matches what seems to be the target market's preference. In communicating internally, the employer has a captive market, but this does not mean that needs can be taken for granted. Employees are not a homogeneous mass. They have a range of skills and expertise, preferences and prejudices, ignorance and experience. Those preferences and requirements must be taken account of in designing adequate communications – a point which is dealt with in detail in the following chapters. This point is also vital in determining an involvement policy.

Involvement policy

The main joint interest of management and employees revolves around the success and continuation of the employing entity. Indeed, one can argue that this is one of the main reasons for embarking on active communication – to unlock the ideas and input of those whose activities can make or mar the success of the organisation. In such a case it may be advisable to set out how it is envisaged such a practice working.

EMPLOYEE INVOLVEMENT PROCEDURE

1 Corporate attitude

(a) The organisation recognises the individual importance of every employee and will seek to ensure that, at all times, such employees are well informed concerning the activities and plans of the organisation, to a degree which does not endanger the development or marketing of its products, services, etc.

(b) The organisation wishes to encourage the development of all employees to the level of attainment with which they are satisfied and will seek to inform, coach and train employees at all times.

(c) The organisation recognises that its aims will be most effectively achieved by involving employees in decisions and developments, and will endorse and encourage all means by which this can be sought.

(d) The organisation recognises that in a rapidly changing world, particularly in employment, traditional attitudes will not suffice, and there is a continual need to address the means by which labour can be acquired and retained, which will require flexibility and innovation.

(e) The organisation supports the concept, principles and practice of the 'Investors in People' initiative and abides by its guidelines.

(f) The organisation commits itself to the following procedures:

    (i)   to maintain an attractive pay and reward package;

    (ii) to maintain a modern progressive personnel policy;

    (iii) to maintain a flexible approach to employment problems;

    (iv) to ensure those with special skills are paid an appropriate premium to reflect those skills;

(v) to review and reward extra effort and performance;

(vi) to examine all jobs to see if there are other ways in which they can be performed;

(vii) to examine all recruitment sources;

(viii) to examine all training programmes;

(ix) to forge links with the education system;

(x) to keep an open mind concerning problems and solutions, and to approach challenges inventively;

(xi) to try to grant to employees a chance to build a capital stake in the organisation.

2 Relationship with community, sponsorship and recruitment

The organisation will continue to be a member of the Business in the Community movement, and to support other local initiatives, encouraging its employees to join in the schemes enhancing the environment within which we operate, by means of day and block release or secondment, and encourages the communication of the results of such work to other employees. In recruiting employees it will ensure that appointments are made solely on the basis of suitability for the vacancy, requires that there be no discrimination against applicants on grounds of sex, race, religion, colour, disability or union membership or non-membership, and that no employee should conduct such discrimination against another employee. Wherever possible the organisation will recruit from within, subject to the appropriate level of skills, experience and aptitude being available.

3 Appointment

On appointment a new employee will receive the items as set out in the communication policy to the content of which the attention of all employees is drawn.

New employees will be introduced to their colleagues and environment by their manager, will be supervised under the mentoring scheme for their first eight weeks' employment and will attend an induction course during that period.

4 During employment, each employee will receive the items as set out in the communication policy

5 General commitment

All levels of management are expected and encouraged to keep their employees informed of all activities and developments in an informal manner in addition to the formal methods set out in this policy, it being recognised that there is no substitute for face-to-face, two-way communication. Senior management will visit every facility and department regularly, endeavouring to talk informally to as many employees as possible.

Employees are encouraged to take a lively interest in the activities of the organisation and, should there be anything on which they have insufficient information or concerning which they are unsure, are encouraged to ask their immediate superior and, should they not receive an adequate answer, to pursue their query through the grievance procedure set out in the employee handbook. Both parties are urged to listen, with an open mind, to the other to ensure an active dialogue is achieved, to ensure misunderstandings are explained and to ensure a unity of purpose.

6 Continuous development

The organisation wishes to encourage its employees to develop their natural talents for mutual benefit. There will be regular joint performance review sessions between employees and manager when performance, aims, problems etc. will be discussed in order to ensure the attainment of continuous development via training geared to the individual needs of each employee.

7 Discipline

The organisation expects employees to act in accordance with preset rules and normal standards of behaviour, and appreciates that most employees do act in such a way most of the time. Where exceptions to this role occur, it may be necessary for disciplinary action to be taken. The disciplinary and grievance procedures have been formulated to deal with such transgressions fairly and objectively in accordance with the rules of natural justice.

67

The requirement to prepare for the added dimension envisaged by an involvement policy should not be lightly dismissed, as current draft European Union (EU) legislation could require public companies to implement such policies. Unfortunately, while the commitment is sound it is another two pages of words for everyone to read. There may be an argument for combining the communication and involvement policies, and incorporating the aims or mission statement in the same document. To a large extent the words themselves hardly matter, other than as a criteria and a conduit for action. Stating their policies in this area is helpful, but carrying out the commitment in practice is what really counts. In *The Nice Company* (Bloomsbury, 1990), Tom Lloyd argues that it is increasingly necessary for companies to adopt 'nice' policies in their dealings with their employees because such policies work. 'People are the key to competitive advantage', Lloyd argues, and being a 'nice' company means having a willingness to think long term, to value reputation and to build partnerships. One cannot think long term without aims, one cannot value reputation without embracing quality and one cannot build a partnership without communicating.

6

Face to face

'Councils of war'

Key learning points

1 **The appropriate form of communication for each situation needs to be determined**
2 **Before attempting to give a briefing or presentation, training should be undertaken**
3 **Top management briefings may be preferable to 'cascade' to ensure a unified message and authoritative responses**
4 **Employees may need to be introduced to the process of briefing to ensure the full benefits are attained**

In 1994 Sir John Harvey Jones defined the following as the three characteristics of a good leader.

- **To have vision.** 'You have got to have a clear view as to where you want to take whatever it is you have got.'

- **To be able to communicate.** 'Frankly the ability to listen is the rarest of characteristics. Listening is all about what people don't say. It is only in Britain where dead silence means either assent or violent dissent.'

- **To be robust.** 'Sheer robustness, both mentally and physically. I mean Nelson kept on losing bits of himself and there was only about a quarter of him left by the time he ended.' It is perhaps worth highlighting that Nelson 'ended' as he was winning his finest victory in which, until struck down, he had led from the front in full view of, and experiencing the same dangers as, his men, while one of his messages 'England expects' lives on as a classic example of excellent communication.

To manage, motivate and lead employees means talking to, listening to and communicating with them. Sadly, often this essential responsibility is shirked by managers seemingly unwilling to take up the position of managing the activities of those who report to them – preferring indeed to 'get on with their own work'. The fact that there is a leadership vacuum and that no one may actually be 'managing' does not necessarily mean that nothing will be done. Almost certainly, however, it will mean that priorities are not correctly determined, and standards of performance and services are lower than is required. The responsibility of managers is to make things happen in accordance with a predetermined scheme, using their employees as the means by which those requirements are attained. The practice of management is essentially proactive – managers must be people who can make things happen. Management cannot afford to assume that employees are aware of the situation. They may have a reasonable idea of the facts, but lacking input, or a full appreciation of the circumstances, can make the wrong conclusions, or assume the wrong priorities or situation.

70

Case study 6.1
NEVER ASSUME

The management could not understand why morale seemed so low when there was every indication that bumper sales figures would be achieved in the immediate future. To cope with the additional demand, stocks of finished product had been built, and were being stored in both in-house and external stores. The employees, used to seeing the stockroom around half full, had assumed that sales were well down and the stockpiling was due to poor demand. Since no one had briefed the employees on the anticipated upturn, the wrong conclusion had been assumed, and at a time when the company needed high morale and commitment.

Key technique
They say that if you 'assume' it only makes an 'ass' of 'u' and 'me'. Only if the correct messages are communicated can we generate the correct response.

'Getting the message across'

In order to ensure everyone is working towards a common aim with set priorities, as well as to avoid the type of classic misunderstanding instanced in case study 6.1, management needs to invest time, constantly briefing and updating those whose efforts are needed to achieve the aims that have been determined. This degree of comprehension can only be effected by a regular and reliable process, usually referred to under the above, somewhat misleading, heading. It is true that messages need to be 'got across', but this is essentially the purveying or promotion of information. Of far greater value is the creation of a dialogue and actually listening to those doing the work.

Case study 6.2
IT'S THE WRONG BUCKET

Quality of product was erratic and constantly referred to in cascade briefing sessions. At one such session the director responsible for corporate communications sat in and heard the usual exhortations that more care was needed to ensure quality was maintained on a regular basis. Considerable discussion ensued concerning the elusive reasons for the variation in quality, during which the director heard one supervisor comment that it was because they were using the wrong bucket. This was apparently an 'in-joke' and the supervisor's comment received a humorous response. The director sought further details and found that, for convenience, the standard measure for one ingredient of the product was a 'bucketful'. However, the bucket that had previously been used had been galvanised steel and the operator had used the rivets as her measurement criteria. The steel bucket had been replaced by a plastic bucket of slightly different dimensions to the old. In addition, it had no rivets. Thus, the operator was guessing the quantity of the ingredient – sometimes accurately and sometimes not.

Key technique
Constant policing of procedures and practices is essential to ensure maintenance of standards.

71

In seeking to develop a rapport in order to ensure everyone is working to the same end, various means must be employed. These will differ and should be geared to the particular circumstances required. Face-to-face communication with Number 1 is extremely effective but virtually impossible to achieve on a regular basis other than in smaller organisations. Almost inevitably we need to employ less effective methods.

Communication

1 Verbal (which includes the use of TV and video)

(a) briefings from top management

(b) briefings from own direct management/supervision who have previously been briefed by top management (the cascade system)

(c) workplace forums

(d) formal meetings

(e) quality circles.

2 Written

(a) formal reports

(b) newsletters and journals

(c) information sheets

(d) memos and/or notices.

Briefings

All verbal encounters require input from a leader and a few guidelines on making a presentation are appropriate. The overriding rule should be to place oneself in the position of the recipients and to try to assess one's presentation through their eyes, bearing in mind that all distractions should be avoided.

Case study 6.3
KEYS LOCK OUT ATTENTION

The chairman was used to commanding attention and experienced in chairing board meetings. He was not, however, used to speaking to a number of people within a more formal context. At a conference, at which he had to give the keynote presentation, he was very nervous. This nervousness manifested itself in a habit of keeping his left hand in his trouser pocket constantly fingering a set of keys. The sound of these keys jingling was such a distraction to the audience that the impact of his words was lost. During the coffee break the discussion was more about the keys than about the content!

> **Key technique**
> *If unused to this kind of exercise, practice is advisable in order to spot such unwelcome habits prior to eradicating them.*

The person in charge of the briefing must control it, and be seen to control it, with firmness, tact and humour. The rules set out below should be used as a guide.

Guidelines for presentation

- Stand in a relaxed manner. In this way it is physically easy to speak and you will command attention.

- Present without a jacket. While in some instances this may be inappropriate, normally it will indicate to those present that you mean business. This is also important to employees not used to attending such functions, as the perceived informality may help them relax.

- Make eye contact. While this can be difficult with more than, say, 40 present, eye contact creates rapport and enables the speaker to check receptivity. If you can see that eyes are becoming glazed or puzzled you may be able to recap and attempt to make the point more clearly, while if they become closed, an attention gainer may be needed. 'Accidentally' dropping a heavy object, or knocking over your coffee cup, does wonders for regaining attention!

- Arrange the room as unlike a classroom as possible. Curved or horseshoe-like layouts are preferable to straight rows. No person should be more than 25 ft from the speaker.

- Ask all delegates to write their forenames on nameplates to be placed in front of them. If a delegate poses a question, the speaker should then be able to use their name to aid the creation of rapport and informality.

- Humour should be used with discretion. Making employees laugh both relaxes them and makes them inhale oxygen, restoring their attention and preventing drowsiness. Conversely, too much laughter may belittle the presentation. However, we learn best when we are relaxed and may only respond in similar circumstances. Since humour aids relaxation it can assist.

- Avoid distractions, both personal and within the room. Windows should be masked if they open on to an area which can provide distractions. The briefing room should not have a telephone, while visitors and interruptions, as well as any extraneous noise, should be avoided.

- The room should be neither too hot nor too cold. Smoking should not be allowed. Water and/or juice should be provided.

- Ensure you can see all those present and that they can all see you. Provide notes so that delegates should only have to write their own amplifying comments and will be able to concentrate on what is said.

- Simplicity should be the watchword, with jargon avoided or at least explained. Notes should be prepared and arranged in order of presentation so that everything proceeds smoothly. Nothing causes embarrassment or disruption more than the speaker being unable to find their place. Similarly, all aids and handouts should also be arranged in order.

- With smaller groups, distributing handouts of particular importance during the session can aid rapport between speaker and delegates. It should also assist the break up of any formality of the session, as well as concentrating the attention on the particular item. Movement attracts attention.

74

- Logical progression of content is essential, with appropriate links between subjects. If the order of content is disrelated, employees may become confused and if they are confused their attention will wander. Ease of familiarity with the subject matter is all important.

- Use visual aids to complement the presentation and to encourage attentiveness. All equipment, computer display, video, slide projector, overhead projector and so on, should be checked out and alternatives made available so that if there is a failure the disruption can be minimised. If all else fails there should always be a flip chart. Don't overuse the equipment, however – it should add interest and complement the content without overwhelming it.

- Invite questions and comments. Again, this will aid rapport and enable you to check that the points have been taken on board by those present. Answer questions as honestly as possible and, if asked a question to which you do not know the answer, say so and promise to get back to the questioner having checked the point out. Honesty will be respected – trying to 'con' or 'flannel' is usually obvious.

- Take questions during the presentation, not at the end. This will encourage employees to regard the briefing as more of a conversation and less of a formal meeting.

- In larger groups, recognise that some may be inhibited from posing questions verbally – either through a fear of speaking publicly or through a fear that the question will be regarded as 'silly'. In these circumstances, encourage the use of written questions, providing pads for the purpose.

■ At the outset stress the invitation to join in and, above all, make the point that the 'silliest' question is the one that isn't asked!

Briefings from top management

The concept of the briefing system is that a checklist of information is generated on a regular basis and used as a base for a presentation by a senior manager to the workforce or their representatives. Obviously, with an organisation of any size this entails splitting the workforce or representatives into manageable groups – probably not exceeding 50. If the senior manager concerned can see all the groups there is a considerable advantage in that essentially the same message should be given to each group. Further, if questions and comments are encouraged, each presentation should benefit from the experience of those preceding, as questions common to more than one group (and possibly not foreseen by the speaker) can be addressed. Indeed, only if such briefings generate feedback and questions will they be really effective. The problem with this method is that it requires a time commitment from a senior manager, although it can be argued that the benefits in terms of demonstrating top management commitment to the process, thereby generating interest and commitment, far outweigh the underlying costs.

75

Preserving the line of command

Where the presentation is to be given by senior management or any level above that to which the employees report, it is essential to try to involve the employees' own managers in the presentation. This will help overcome any suggestion that the line management is being sidestepped or their authority impaired. This can be effected by asking the line manager to introduce the speaker, giving him or her planted comments which show that they are party to the presentation and avoiding answering questions that imply criticism of local management. During the presentation referring operational questions to local management and, at the conclusion, thanking the local management for the opportunity to address their staff can also help.

The advantage for top management carrying out such briefings is that the reaction of the workforce to developments, and particularly to changes, can be gained at first hand without either being sanitised or screened by intervening layers of management. Ideally, no doubt, Monty would have preferred not to have had to use his liaison officers and to speak directly to the half a million under his command. Speaking direct would have given him, as it can senior management, an immediate insight into the reaction of employees within the briefing environment. Hostility, indifference or even apathy then evinced may be indicative of departmental problems, particularly if other groups have no such reaction. Thus, top management will be made aware to a greater and more accurate extent, of the true reactions of the workforce; while the workforce should have demonstrated for them top management's interest in their views.

Case study 6.4
LESS OF LESS

In attempting to explain the relationship of added value, to which a company productivity scheme was tied, to the profit stated in the annual report, the director stated that 'Added value less wages equals the profit'. One supervisor got agitated thinking that the director was advocating that wages should be less (that is lessened or reduced) in order to improve profit. It took some time as well as the use of the word 'minus' to explain the point!

Key technique
The language one uses can mean different things to different people. Jargon, buzz words and complex terminology should always be avoided – but at least when face to face, the speaker has the chance to explain. This is denied if the written word has to be used.

Cascade briefings

The principle and practice of the cascade method of briefing is advocated by several leading companies, having been pioneered by the Industrial Society. The idea is that top management brief middle management, who brief junior management, who brief supervision, who brief the workforce. The briefing needs to be supported by a briefing note prepared centrally and used by all involved. Although this spreads the time commitment from one or two at the top to all management and involves all tiers of management in the process (which may prove very beneficial), it does have a number of potential problems. First, all those involved in briefing need to be trained or coached in the process. Although the principles may be quickly learned, some of the data being dealt with may be entirely too complex for ease of handling by relatively junior or inexperienced personnel. Their capacity for dealing with questions (generating which is, after all, the whole point of the process) may also be strictly limited. The effect may be to put such personnel in the hot seat. This is extremely unfair on everyone involved as it virtually guarantees that they will not do it particularly well – or enjoy doing it, which is vital if it is to be done successfully. The fact that a multiplicity of people are involved in giving out the messages also entails the risk of message confusion – different groups may hear (or think they hear) different messages.

Of course, using the cascade itself can reduce the amount of information flowing in both directions. It is not impossible for 10 per cent of the message to be lost at each level. If this occurs, and there are five levels between the original top management briefer and those at the sharp end, then only around 60 per cent of the message will eventually find its way to the target, while as we saw in case study 4.2, both tone and import can be completely altered. If this distortion works in both directions the answer received by Number 1, when a message has run from top floor to shop floor, and a reply has run the opposite way, may be so distorted as to be nonsensical. If in answer to the fabled 'send three and fourpence we're going to a dance' received by headquarters, the (at least logical) reply 'Wages not received yet, stay where you are' would no doubt mystify the field commander who originally asked for reinforcements so that he could advance. (Of course by the time he received it the message would probably have been recast as 'Cages not relieved yet, stay in your car' – providing still further mystification!)

77

In dealing with the information flowing in the other direction, supervision may well screen out observations, comments and even complaints which they perceive to be critical of their own position or performance. This was exactly what Montgomery feared and used his liaison officers to try to circumvent.

The briefing sheet

Common to both briefing systems is the need to generate a briefing sheet which must be made available to the briefers and may be made available to all being briefed as a record of what was said. Although some organisations fight shy of giving out briefing sheets (understandably in the case of publicly listed companies where the information may include what could be construed as price-sensitive material), the wide dissemination of such items does assist the avoidance of misinterpretations of information. The briefing sheet could be set out as shown below.

DRAFT BRIEFING SHEET

Organisation   *Briefing sheet Ref. Number...........*

Date prepared   *Briefing to be completed by (date)*

1 Company position

   To (date of subject period) sales are ... [up] on budget, profits are ... [up] on budget.

2 Orders

   The order book is satisfactory with ... weeks' orders in house. Special information (general news of particular orders, special interest, etc.)

3 Promotional activity

   News of product developments, new launch reactions, advertising campaigns

4 Production information – productive units achieved compared with budget, downtime, lost time, quality – achieved and problems. Anticipated demand in productive terms etc.

5 Personnel information – system changes. New state requirements etc.

6 Health and safety matters.

7 Other general information.

8 Contacts for further information/answers to questions raised at previous briefings.

If the practice of handing out copies to those attending the briefings has been adopted, then there may be a provision to pose written questions either for answer at a subsequent briefing (as allowed under point 8 above) or direct to an individual, or, if the answer has more general interest, in an internal newsletter.

Introducing briefing

It is essential, no matter what kind of briefing is anticipated, either management or cascade, or indeed briefing via workplace forums, quality circles, etc., as described below, that those responsible for conducting the briefing are themselves coached and given guidance on how to operate the system. While some are instinctive presenters and 'briefers', most do require coaching and support as they tend to see the system as ego questioning. Below is set out an outline introductory note used to introduce the concept of team briefing to Filofax PLC. This version of the team briefing concept addressed not just the idea of team building by discussing workplace problems, but linked with it the company suggestion scheme (requiring the employees to consider suggestions made by their own team members) and the productivity bonus scheme (suggesting that employees consider in groups, as well as individually, ideas for improving productivity), which were considered priorities at that time of the company's development. To some extent the actual content required to be considered, and/or the circumstances of the meeting, are unimportant. The fact that the team and the team leader are talking to each other, and, because they are talking, they are achieving a greater understanding of each other's problems and aspirations, is the real aim and benefit of the whole process.

INTRODUCING A BRIEFING SYSTEM

Team meetings

Objectives:

1 To bind the working team together by discussing problems to arrive at possible solutions.

2 To discuss and approve/reject suggestions made under the suggestion scheme.

3 To provide a formal communication channel to discuss items of mutual interest.

Method:

1 Monthly meeting led by the supervisor/manager attempting to be as informal as practical.

2 Team leader needs to prepare by

   (a) listing problems for team consideration

   (b) considering suggestions made

   (c) arranging for a team member to take notes and to have these available at subsequent meetings

   (d) having available company briefing.

3 Team leader must ensure all questions raised and noted and answered either during meeting or subsequently if the information is not immediately available. (Note that answers will be provided unless this would breach confidentiality, in which case this will be stated.)

4 Team leader should ensure sufficient time allowed for discussion of items. Meetings will not normally last more than 30–45 minutes.

Team leader preparation:

1 Collect news from own and other departments (arrange exchange with team leaders from linked departments).

2 Familiarise yourself with the content of the company briefing obtaining answers to anticipated questions.

3 Collect suggestions made from those in the team, consider objectively, list problems and advantages but do not pre-judge – let team discuss and come to its own conclusion(s).

4 Check that all questions raised at previous meeting have been answered and, if not, obtain/prepare answers for team.

5 List all items for consideration in a checklist for reference during the meeting to ensure nothing is overlooked.

Running the meeting:

1 Three essentials – prepare, prepare, prepare!

2 Remember that the meeting is purely a conversation such as you might have at the workplace. Try not to be nervous – it is just an informal chat with the aim of trying to understand each other's viewpoints, problems and aims.

3 Forget about yourself – concentrate on the business you want to get through (from your checklist) and ensure team members have a fair hearing.

4 Be enthusiastic – only if you are will the team be.

5 Encourage all to participate. If certain members are shy or not forth-coming, try to involve them by asking them by name whether they agree or disagree with items. Some employees will speak up without encour-agement, others require a great deal of encouragement. Help those who have difficulty expressing themselves by putting a version of what you think they are saying in your own words and then checking with them that you have it right.

6 Stress that although the team needs to hear of complaints the idea is to solve such complaints, not just to give an opportunity for a grumble ses-sion. Suggest that anyone having a complaint should also have a sug-gestion as to how it can be resolved.

7 Don't suggest that all problems have an immediate answer – or that the team should know all the answers. If there is a question without an answer, refer back to line management to try to find the answer and let the team know this at the next meeting.

8 Summarise the discussion and decisions before closing the meeting. Ensure any members who have been asked to carry out tasks know this.

9 Set the date for the next briefing.

10 If required to cancel the team briefing meeting: don't.
(Note: If it is absolutely impossible to hold the briefing at the date/time stated, then postpone the meeting by no more than two working days, but never cancel even if there seems little to discuss. The success of the dialogue depends upon regularity of meeting, and cancellation will destroy the trust in the system and thus the concept itself – the impression will be given that the process is unimportant. If there is little to discuss, then keep the meeting short – remember that, in any case, you will have the company briefing to refer to, and that this, in turn, may generate comment and/or question.)

Communicating using meetings

'Sending signals'

Key learning points

1 Speakers at communication meetings need to be trained
2 Since some employees may feel very concerned at attending such an event, reassurance and persuasion may be needed
3 Chairmen may need to encourage members to participate
4 Workplace forums and quality circles may be more conducive than formal meetings to ensure participation.

If the phrase 'take minutes and waste hours' can be accurately applied to your meetings then obviously there is something wrong – possibly that the aims and purpose have not been clearly identified and communicated to those present. With meetings involving employees who may not be used to this format, it is essential that the purpose is determined well in advance, as well as being stated at the outset of the meeting itself. This should help avoid confusion.

Case study 7.1
IT'S NOT ABOUT ME THEN?

The company had won national awards for the clarity of its corporate communication material which sought to explain in laymen's terms the financial results of the previous year to non-financially oriented employees. At the end of one briefing group held to discuss the employee report, when asked if there were any more questions, one employee asked when they would be discussing her progress. She was a newcomer and, when invited to a session on an 'employee report', had been under the impression that what would be discussed would be her, and other employees', progress since recruitment.

Key technique
The objectives of every meeting need to be made crystal clear in advance to all involved.

In setting up such events we need to prepare

- the chairman
- the speakers
- the attendees
- the venue, and
- the data

to ensure that the event does not 'come across' as management preaching to the assembled throng, but more as a meeting of several viewpoints from which can emerge consensus or, if not, then at least comprehension of differing viewpoints. Very often the reaction to the invite is that it will simply waste time that could be utilised productively. If the numbers attending exceed 40/50, then there may be little opportunity for two-way interaction which means that there may be little feeling of involvement by the delegates. Conversely, if the chairman or speaker is an extrovert then some of these shortcomings may be overcome.

83

The chairman

It may be initially thought that the type of meetings envisaged here do not need a chairman as such, but nevertheless without someone in control of the event, speakers may ramble without control. Chairmanship relies a great deal on personality to carry both business and members along, pushing the meeting to the point where its aims are achieved. The chairman needs to have:

- vision, to move the meeting towards aims attainment;
- good communication skills so that his or her vision is communicated to other members, and;
- enthusiasm to motivate members so that they learn to believe in plans and ideas, and, where appropriate, in their own ability to perform and achieve them.

Case study 7.2
LAYING IT ON THE LINE

The chairman in his opening address to the quality circle not only welcomed everyone but stated that the circle would be run as informally as possible. However, this would be matched by a need for total accountability and commitment. He added that he only wanted people to attend the circle who were prepared to operate under those guidelines and invited anyone not prepared to do so to leave it. No one moved.

Key technique
Making a public declaration can act as considerable peer pressure on all present and also, in this case, underlined the basis of the concept.

The three aspects of good chairmanship set out above need to be exerted at all times during a meeting in order to move it forward. In doing this the chairman is essentially manipulating the members as well as the meeting itself. In fact this may not be difficult since if employees can identify with a successful effort they tend to co-operate and work more effectively. If they have something of which they can be proud, and know that their contribution is important to the meeting and the organisation, they tend to commit to a far greater degree than may otherwise be the case. In any event basic involvement tends to create an environment where individuals work willingly – the PIE circle is at work again.

Each of these aspects of controlling those present infers that the chairman will motivate the members, for example, by the judicious use of praise or by encouraging them to bring to the meeting certain problems for discussion and assistance. The success or otherwise of the meeting depends very much on the effectiveness of the chairman, whose duties and responsibilities are outlined below.

Responsibilities of a chairman

- To take responsibility for pushing the meeting itself to consider all its business, but only its business, and to attain its aims.

- To be conscious of what is trying to be achieved from each item of business and by the entire meeting.

- To ensure that not only is each item on the agenda dealt with comprehensively, but also that all members are heard on the subject, which may mean actively inviting members to contribute, rather than passively waiting for them to do so. For example, 'Jo, we haven't heard your view – do you have any comments?' Asking this kind of question rather than 'What do you think?' protects the person identified in case they do not have anything to offer or simply prefer not to comment. If put on the spot by the alternative question, the person lacking self-confidence may not simply be tongue-tied, but may seek to avoid coming to the meeting again.

- To bring the meeting back to the business in hand should it stray.

- To close down members' arguments or contentions where these threaten to swamp consideration of the subject matter and are not progressing the discussion. This is particularly relevant if the meeting is subject to a time limit. The problem is that often the value of such members' contribution is in inverse proportion to the amount of time they spend propounding it. Moving the meeting on can, in such circumstances, take considerable tact.

- To ensure the decisions arrived at are recorded and promulgated, and subsequent meetings are arranged.

- To lead the discussion and the meeting itself. A chairman is a leader, and an effective leader is someone who makes things happen and achieves results through people. The required work of the chairman is thus to seek to make things happen through the members.

85

Motivating members

The role of chairman combines that of being 'first among equals' with that of leader and this dual role should always be recognised. In the latter endeavour the chairman should ensure the best of each member is brought out within the meeting. Without the chairman's control, it may be easy for a dominant person to take over the meeting and for less dominant members to be overshadowed to such an extent that they make little or no contribution. It is the chairman's responsibility to encourage the quieter members to make a contribution, even, if necessary, silencing others in order for them to do so. In this the chairman will need to adopt the guidelines set out below.

Meeting guidelines

- Ensure everyone knows why they are present. In this the chairman may need to restate the meeting's objectives and may also state the time within which he or she would like to see the business conducted. Such strictures must be promoted positively, the aim being to complete the business properly, recognising that time is scarce and valuable.

- Treat every member as an individual with rights to make the points he or she wishes. This may require the chairman actually inviting a contribution by name from the 'less forward' members.

- Encourage every member to identify with the body as a whole and to relate to every other member. This will take time and, with some members, can be difficult.

- Encourage a sense of pride in the meeting and its achievements. Without being effusive, the chairman should praise achievements whether these be joint or individual. In the UK people tend to criticise too much and praise too little. Praise is also helpful when trying to manipulate a meeting, since the 'feel good' effect can stifle or neutralise what could otherwise be objections. In the UK, success often seems to embarrass and achievements even tend to be denigrated, despite success itself being a powerful motivator.

- Ensure all members are treated fairly, and given a chance both to explain their views and attitudes, and to argue their case. Obviously this in turn requires the opposition to have a chance to do the same. If members see that each is allowed his or her own turn to put forward arguments, the temptation to use means by which the arguments of others are not heard (for example wasting time on trivialities) should be reduced.

- Ensure members see that business which they feel is important does get discussed. This may be difficult in the early life of a meeting and the chairman needs to be tactful in accepting or rejecting business requested by members. If it is entirely germane to the business in hand, it may be worth considering, even if that in turn means the meeting overruns its allotted time span. If it is not appropriate, a tactful suggestion, 'Perhaps we could have an initial chat about that after the meeting', might solve the problem without disincentivising the member.

The speaker

The guidelines on making an effective presentation set out in Chapter 6 should be the starting point, since very often the way information is presented and delivered is every bit as valuable as the content of the information. A good presentation may be able to compensate for poorly prepared material, but a poor presentation will always reflect badly on the content no matter how well prepared it may be. Those who are to speak need to familiarise themselves with both the content to be addressed and those who will be present. Where input is expected from those present, the presentational material must be presented in a way to which those present will find it easy to relate – data must be user-friendly. Speakers not used to having to deliver in such a forum should be encouraged to practise their delivery and to learn how to deal with the 'audience'.

Attendees

To many employees, having to attend meetings or briefings may be something of an ordeal. Not familiar with the requirements of the format, they become fearful, and not used to expressing themselves in such a meeting, they may spend all their time trying to look inconspicuous and to avoid any request to contribute. These are natural fears and must not be dismissed as unimportant or trivial, since to the person involved they are anything but. The challenge is really how to reassure those with such fears, since if the aim is to gain input from the audience, and if several are suffering from a similar reticence, the effectiveness of the discussion will be lost. Presumably Henry V well understood this reticence – hence him disguising himself to obtain his followers' views in an informal manner, not one circumscribed by the trappings of power and position. Recognising the problem is half the battle – the other half is combating it, in which case an informal note, such as that set out below may assist.

87

Dear [Name]

On [date] we are holding a meeting to discuss how our team can improve output and quality. I know from our previous discussions that you are keen that these aspects of our operation should receive attention. This discussion provides a good opportunity for all of us jointly to explore our ideas aimed at improving output and procedures.

We intend that it should be as informal a gathering as possible, but to cater for everyone this will mean that there will be around 30 present. Although this is a large number, apart from [director], all those present will be your own colleagues.

I hope you will be able to come along and, if you have ideas, put these forward for discussion. I know you can be somewhat reticent about putting your ideas forward, and if instead you would like a colleague or I to make your suggestions, please let me know. I am particularly concerned that should any of your ideas be accepted you should receive both recognition and any reward, and in these circumstances it would certainly be preferable if you were to speak yourself.

Perhaps we can discuss this before the meeting.

Yours, etc.

Alternatively, since even the attempted informality of such a note may concern some not used to dealing with the written word, a quiet informal chat along the same lines may be more beneficial. Reassurance is the name of the game and suggesting that a less inhibited colleague discuss things with and accompany the introverted employee may assist.

Data

The preparation and presentation of data is dealt with in later chapters, but in terms of its preparation for use by meeting members, particularly those not used to handling such items, it is essential to register that it should be presented in a user-friendly way – that is in a form and format to which those present can easily relate. 'Never underestimate intelligence but never overestimate knowledge' is a sound maxim in this regard, since most people are quite capable of understanding the most complex information, provided it is presented in a format to which they can relate and which they can understand. Thus all data (indeed all material for communication) should avoid jargon and use plain ordinary language. Written text should be presented in a way that will attract the average reader and retain attention thereafter. This is not to say that internal documents need the attentions of professional designers, but that the text should be prepared with care, with use made of headlines, illustrations and photographs, as well as graphics, particularly where figures are being reviewed. The eye perceives pages as a picture and most people find it much easier to derive information from text which is augmented by good illustrations.

The impression of a text-filled page is of a mass of grey – uninteresting and unattractive – which can be made immeasurably worse if a small type size is used. Many readers instinctively distrust small type (which can in any case be difficult to read), feeling that it is used only because someone has something to hide. Interestingly, it is illegal for pawnbrokers to use too small a font size in documentation which will be used by their borrowers! If the aim is to achieve receptivity of the message, the medium itself must be constructed in a way that ensures the recipient can accept and understand it. This should be so obvious that it should not need repeating and yet originators of data constantly overlook the point.

Case study 7.3
MISING THE POINT

Each year public companies are required to present to their owners – the shareholders – a report on their financial and other activities. These tend to be expensive, professionally produced documents, yet research indicates that only about 5 per cent of the shareholders (the target audience for the document) actually read and understand the content. In its book *Making Corporate Accounts Valuable* (Kogan Page, 1988), the Chartered Institute of Accountants in Scotland stated that such accounts were often so complex that they were capable of being understood only by their authors.

Key technique
Content must always be related to the interests and requirements of the target audience.

Workplace forums

89

The structure of the workplace forum is far less formal than either of the briefing concepts described in Chapter 6, but may be more akin to what was described as 'Team briefing' at Filofax. A forum entails a gathering of the natural working group in a meeting chaired by the group supervisor, with the aim of discussing primarily work and workplace problems, although forum discussion can often spill over into more general areas. If this occurs the supervisor may need to obtain more information or guidance from another source or manager, who may be invited to attend a subsequent meeting.

The process depends very much on the character and approach of the supervisor. Inexperienced or insecure supervisors may well need coaching, and possibly support, in order to ensure the group's potential for garnering all constituent parts of the team to the required aims is attained. Although described as a meeting, such a session tends to be (and ideally should be) far less formal than would be generally understood by the term and less formal than briefings. Such forums are best held at or near the workplace itself, provided there is an area where it can be held in reasonable comfort and quiet. The familiarity of locale and of being with working colleagues may be of assistance to less forthcoming or reticent employees, who may find great difficulty in playing any part or asserting themselves in a larger group.

The problems for management are ensuring that:

- the forums take place regularly and the time allocated is used to move problems forward, not simply as a time when a good chin-wag can be enjoyed by all at the employer's expense;
- subject material is discussed objectively and constructively;
- everybody is encouraged to speak their mind; and
- each individual's views are sought and carefully considered.

With insecure or ill-prepared supervisors, it is sometimes the case that either excuses are found which ensure that the forums do not take place (which can also be a problem with cascade briefings) or the forums are constantly postponed until they are 'forgotten about'. It may be wise when setting up such a system to make a proviso that the next line of management 'drops in' on the forum once every three or four months and that there is some kind of independent feedback from those taking part. Irrespective of the form or level of policing the system, the supervisor should be required to report to the next line manager and/or to the senior manager with overall responsibility for the concept, noting any decision (or disputes) and any action taken by the group or required from a source external to the group. In addition, any questions etc., raised by the group which could not be answered immediately must be relayed for answering – either direct or via through the group at its following forum.

Quality circles

The forum type of exchange is often used in organisations adopting the quality circle concept where the emphasis is essentially on improving the quality of product, and productive processes and service within pre-set standard requirements. Having determined problem areas, task forces (similar in composition to the work teams used in team briefing above) consider the problem and attempt to improve or resolve it. The system can either be used on a one-off basis or, as is more common, on a continuous basis, either entitled 'task forces' or sometimes 'improvement groups'. Improvement groups can be drawn from a number of different departments (indeed they are often comprised of volunteers) and thus the normal working team environment is blurred, and the problems addressed tend to be those common to a number of areas.

An advantage of this cross-department team composition is that representatives of departments learn more about the operations of other departments and come to appreciate their problems and priorities which may put their own into perspective. Above all else, however, the concept is dependent upon input from both employees and management, and thus, inevitably, communication follows. Those companies that have adopted quality circles almost universally state that considerable benefits have accrued as a result, although, as noted previously, this may be as much a result of the enhanced communication requirement as anything else. Many have moved on to adopt the principles of the quality standard BS 5750 and recent research into the effects of the introduction of that standard suggest that most firms that have introduced the standard have increased their profits as a direct result.

Formal meetings

The principle common to the above versions of briefing is of an active participation by shop-floor employees and, indeed, it is this involvement that is the main constituent of the success of such schemes. However, it is not always possible to arrange small briefings in order to inform employees of particular matters. It may then be necessary to hold virtually formal meetings where the employees attend more as an audience than as participants – required to listen passively to a presentation. Obviously the onus is then placed on the presenter to try, by using good presentational skills (see the Filofax briefing system), enhanced by visual aids (slides, transparencies, video and so on), to first capture and then retain the attention of the audience. Too often, however, management meetings are held with little preparation or consideration of the requirements of the audience.

Nowhere is this lack of attention more likely to result in poor acceptance and retention of the message than in the presentation of figures. Whereas literacy in the UK is poor to the extent that research indicates that one in seven people have difficulty reading, numeracy is even worse. Few people can appreciate the implications of a line of figures and if these are read out, acceptability is virtually nil. Thus, attention must be paid to the manner of presentation of the information and, if figures are to be part of the message to be delivered, bar charts (to demonstrate relative values), pie charts (to demonstrate relative proportions), graphs (to demonstrate movement over a period), and other graphics and illustrations may need to be utilised, with handouts made available for further reference. Most people find it much easier to derive an initial review of financial information from graphics than they do from listed statistics. The limitations of video in this context should be stressed, however. Despite it being essentially a graphical medium, and excellent for presenting images and concepts, video is less effective than printed material if presenting figures and results other than in the most general way. It should not be overlooked that because a meeting may be structured with a large audience, almost inevitably the possibility of feedback is restricted. Leaving sufficient time for questions and using roving microphones may ensure at least the facility for the audience to pose a few questions.

Case study 7.4
THE FORMAL ANNUAL MEETING

NFC (the former National Freight Consortium) is a company where the employees, even after the company's public flotation, still hold a majority of votes attaching to the shares, which they originally acquired at the time of the very successful management buyout. The company holds an employee general meeting and after a brief presentation encourages questions from the floor, which tends to provoke lively debates. The whole process is recorded on video and the video is then made available to employees not able to attend the meeting.

Despite all present at the NFC and similarly owned organisations' meetings having a vested interest in learning all there is to know about the results of the company (after all those attending actually invested their own money in the company), being unused to the format and the formality normally expected at such a meeting can lead some present to behave in a manner which may be regarded by some as not 'in keeping' with such an event. Regardless of its source, or the reason for its occurrence, this can be very disturbing, both to others present whose attention will be distracted, and to the speaker who may find his or her own attention wandering and the calibre of the presentation itself impaired. Such antisocial behaviour can include talking to another delegate, humming or tapping a pencil. The difficulty is that often the person concerned may be virtually unaware of the action or of the effect it is having and could be very embarrassed when it is pointed out to them. The protection of susceptibilities is all-important, particularly where the action is simply a result of not realising the generally accepted manner of behaviour. If a break is near then it may be preferable to wait until the break before quietly and tactfully explaining to the person involved that their actions are causing a problem. Alternatively, it may be necessary to break into the programme with a tactfully worded request to desist.

Case study 7.5
AVOIDING DISTRACTIONS

At a meeting for around 40 employees, two from the same department, sitting in the front row, chatted incessantly and it was obvious to the speaker that, although he was not affected too badly, others present were finding it difficult to concentrate. In inviting questions, the speaker positioned himself so that the chatterers were directly between him and a questioner. He was then able to say to the questioner, 'I'm sorry I can't hear you' and then to the chatterers, 'I'm sorry, I can't hear [name]'s question, which may affect the point you are discussing'. This was followed up by a tactful word during the break.

Key technique
The best means of defence may be attack – and to attack we need to be prepared. Trying to outguess all the problems and conjure solutions can be very effective – at the very least it allows the meeting to proceed smoothly and reflects well on the organisation.

93

8

The power – and responsibilities – of print

'Publish and be damned!'

> **Key learning points**
>
> 1 Written communications lack the immediacy, emphasis and 'tone' of body language; and may pose a problem of permanence
> 2 Notices need careful content framing and their posting must be controlled to ensure effectiveness
> 3 Written data must be carefully examined for simplicity, clarity and brevity
> 4 There needs to be a provision for feedback as the written route does not automatically provide one.

The Duke of Wellington's famous angry retort reproduced above should be taken as a warning to be remembered whenever using the printed format. In face-to-face discussions we can recall or explain words, we can use emphasis and body language to strengthen or soften our message. Indeed, gestures can even become part of the language and aid communication.

Case study 8.1
CAN'T READ HAND SIGNALS OVER THE PHONE

Not being fluent in French the administrator found it difficult to converse with French applicants over the phone, most of whom had similar difficulties speaking English. However, when they actually met, the comprehension difficulties virtually disappeared. 'I can't understand why we can get by now but not when they are on the phone.' 'It's very simple', replied the consultant, 'when you are face to face as much as 40 per cent of effective communication may achieved by body language and mime. This is obviously impossible over the phone.'

Key technique
Those endeavouring to reduce communication data to the written format need to appreciate that they are using a format which is far less effective than verbal and face-to-face communication. Great care needs to be taken to ensure the message conveyed by the words is the message required.

Intriguingly, Desmond Morris recounts in The Human Animal *(BBC Books, 1994) that in Japan, where it is customary to bow when meeting, bows are exchanged even when the parties are conversing by phone!*

On the football touchline the manager's tone, posture and reaction all give messages which can enhance the actual words the manager wishes to hurl at the team on the field. Giving them a note – even incorporating stronger language, bold type, colour or underlining – simply would not have the same impact. Conversely, spoken words (if not the overall sense) can be swiftly forgotten, whereas a note provides permanent evidence of the message given which can be embarrassing.

95

Case study 8.2
ON THE RIGHT TRACK

The 1994 dispute between Railtrack and the signalmen's union occurred while this book was being written. The original negotiations broke down and the first strike was called because an 'offer' of around 5 per cent was 'withdrawn' by the employer. This was initially denied until the union produced a memo which contained the figure referred to.

Key technique
Putting something into print gives it a permanence that words lack. In conversation words can be corrected instantly – or even recalled or denied. This is not possible with written material.

Within organisations there are several forms of written communications that we can use, including

- slogans
- posters
- newspapers, newsletters, journals and magazines
- memos and letters
- bulletins, fact sheets and leaflets
- reports

and the order used may be a fairly accurate guide to the diminishing effectiveness of these as communication tools. Thanks to the wonders of the electronic age we can also use:

- electronic mailboxes (or E-mail), and
- networking.

96 *'One cannot ask questions of a piece of paper'*

In attempting to inform or engender communication face to face and verbally, we have the great advantage of being able to reinforce and even recall our words. Indeed, the very way we say them and the body language we employ provides messages which may be totally at odds with the words used. Taking an extreme example there is a world of difference between hearing the words 'I'm going to kill you' if they are said with a smile in a cheerful and off-hand tone, and if they are ground out between the teeth of a villainous stranger in an aggressive pose, with a gun in his hand. In these instances the actual words used may be identical, but body language has either destroyed the literal meaning and suggested that this is all a joke, or has reinforced it.

In delivering a number of presentations at conferences and seminars each year, I sometimes realise I have used an inaccurate word or phrase. Instantly, I have the opportunity to recall the word and substitute alternative(s). The mistake will be excused as a slip of the tongue or simply ignored by most delegates and the new word(s) will be substituted without another thought. The sense I wished to convey has been created – albeit at a second attempt. The use of the wrong word may even be an excuse for a little humour which aids rapport and provides a break from concentration. Correcting ourselves in this way indicates we are thinking about the content. However, it is virtually impossible to correct ourselves when we use the written word. The words we write are there for all to see and, if we have used the wrong word, it can be extremely difficult to eradicate it. The problem may be all the greater if the mistaken printed word is at all emotive. In this case it may create all sorts of unwanted reactions, none of which, as the author is not present, may be capable of correction. In dialogue, if we do not understand, we can ask for clarification, and the wise respondent to such a request will tend to use other words having a similar meaning to try to convey the original sense. Paper messages provide us with no such opportunity, so great thought needs to be given to how we actually frame our words and how we display them on the page or paper.

Case study 8.3
WHAT DO YOU MEAN?

The organisation had experienced a problem with the production of an internal directory and found, after it had been dispatched, that a number of copies had blank pages. It sent out the following memo :

> A spot check of randomly selected directories indicates that a number of such directories contain several blank pages. In view of the foregoing it is suggested that each user review his or her directory and ascertain whether or not the directory contains blank pages. In the event the directory is incomplete the user should return the directory to source for disposition.

Key technique

1. *For some reason the writer dispensed with normal English and retreated (possibly as a defence mechanism because of the mistake) into some kind of 'formal reportspeak' language. However, the effect is to confuse the reader.*

2. *Irrelevant information is provided. How the error was discovered is of no significance to the user with a faulty directory. What the 'source' ('Isn't that something I put on my food?') going to do with the returned directories is immaterial.*

3. *Inappropriate language has been used. To many people the word 'review' could indicate either a musical entertainment or a request to write a critique of the faulty item, while asking them to 'return [it] to source for disposition' could be really confusing.*

4. *It fails the 'What's the point?' test. The point of the item is (presumably) to ensure that the users finish up with faultless directories – which is the one thing the material does not tell them how to obtain!*

Slogans

Presumably what the writer of the piece of gobbledegook in case study 8.3 meant to say was 'If your directory contains blank pages, please send it back to [place] and we will replace it'. However, in dressing up this simple message the words have got in the way of the message. This is the one thing that must never happen with a slogan. The value of slogans has already been stressed. They can encapsulate the theme of the underlying message as well as the message itself. Churchill's 'V-sign' or the chairman's 'It's a pleasure' emulate the mottoes that appear under heraldic coats of arms which try to indicate the philosophy of a family or organisation. 'Nation shall speak peace unto nation' is the motto of the British Broadcasting Corporation, and echoes the aim of the organisation to use communication itself to engender peace and understanding.

Case study 8.4
NORMAN'S HILL

Before it changed its name to that of its product, the company that produces the Filofax was called Norman and Hill Ltd. The chief executive, in introducing a staff incentive scheme, used the punning concept of 'Norman's hill' with a graphical representation of the monthly targets that had to be met to achieve a payout. The real name of the incentive scheme was forgotten – it immediately became 'Norman's hill' which not only identified the scheme but also emphasised the required commitment to a 'climb' or 'effort' to achieve financial reward.

Case study 8.5
BACKFIRING

Introducing a similar scheme to 'Norman's hill', another organisation adopted the three words 'Productivity, Efficiency and Parsimony' to provide the initials of its own 'PEP pill' linked to a productivity reward scheme that had been running for some time. While there was considerable benefit in being able to use the 'PEP pill', particularly graphically in reports, the word 'Parsimony' (only used because no other word really fitted the requirement) provoked a mild backlash from some employees who associated it with 'frugality' or 'meanness'.

Key technique

Despite the backlash and controversy over the use of the word, as the originator of the concept commented, 'At least it means they read and will remember it!' Even disputes and arguments may encourage communication.

Posters

Posters are often used in organisations placed on a notice board as reminders of events, as an exhortation (in which case they will tend to use slogans) for action or (particularly in conjunction with safety matters) to warn of danger. Posters are, or should be, the means of disseminating the simplest form of communication – the message should be clear and simple, and so obvious, that there is no need for question. Perhaps the simplest poster is the advice, 'In case of fire, sound the alarm and evacuate', which few could misunderstand. Obviously any lack of clarity and simplicity will negate the aim of the item. However, all too often the use of the poster is foiled by the use of unclear and complex messages which confuse rather than enlighten, and hamper rather than solve the problems that led to the encounter.

99

Case study 8.6
NOT SO SIMPLE

At an Essex sports centre, the visitor is greeted by a notice which reads 'Please to be advised that you are now entering an area where smoking is not permitted, other than in the confines of the bar'. To be charitable, one assumes the printer was paid by the word and that his business was slack, since 'No smoking – except in the bar' provides a far simpler and more easily understood message. By the same token, presumably that most oft-repeated notice 'Please keep off the grass' would have appeared here as 'Please to be advised that this tended greensward is not to be used underfoot by visitors to this public recreational area'!

Key technique
In this, as in so much that we need to communicate, it is essential to realise that quantity can never substitute for quality. Keep it short and simple – the KISS technique – should be the watchword.

Although the simplest means of imparting information is the adoption of a slogan and posting a notice on a notice board, this does not necessarily ensure receptivity or comprehension. Neither is its posting the end of the matter. To be effective, notices must first be noticed. Used properly, notice boards can be a valuable source of information and can promote communication. However, to do this they need to be sited carefully, not where people pass, as that is what they will do – pass by – but where the target audience is likely to stand. Hence, a busy corridor is probably a less effective site for a notice board than next to the drinks machine or next to the lift doors – or even in the lift. Many hotels advertise their facilities in the lift, knowing (as there are no distractions) that for a few seconds the notice will have the whole attention of the passenger. Wherever sited, however, notices and notice boards must be adequately controlled and managed, an operation which is addressed below.

Notices and notice board administration

A notice is a poster. It needs:

- to capture the eye of the beholder, by displaying a simple message with the aim of instant recognition;
- to be couched in language and terms capable of being understood by the target audience; and
- to provide a contact point for further information or explanation so that any questions generated can be answered.

Other considerations

- Colour is a powerfully attractive force. Thus, using coloured paper for specific types of notices can aid presentational appeal, as well as identifying subject matter – for example, green for safety matters, red for discipline and rules, yellow for benefits and so on.
- Posters rapidly lose their initial impact and eventually become 'unseen' or 'overlooked'. They need to be given a 'shelf life' and to be taken down immediately thereafter. Insisting that all notices bear a 'destruct' date and that they are taken down on or before that destruct date is essential.
- Siting notice boards needs careful consideration. Boards need to be positioned where employees pause, not where they pass.

Categorisation

Notices include:

- those that are required to be displayed by law;
- those that the organisation needs or wishes to display to impart information, or to trigger a response; and
- those that employees (and/or their representatives) may wish to display. Notice boards need to be capable of displaying each of these categories and also need to be administered to ensure the appeal of their content.

Control

- Appoint a person to control boards and the posting of all notices.
- Site boards where employees may pause and read.
- Number each board and then post notices against a numbered checklist to ensure no board is overlooked.
- Keep a master board showing the current 'display' in the office of the notice board controller. Apart from aiding control, this should ensure that there are no conflicting messages generated by different notices.
- Examine content for clarity and accuracy.
- Keep a master file of a copy of each notice posted for reference and to aid preparation of notices in future

101

Distributing notices

If notices are to be distributed rather than posted, for example by means of circulars, many of the above guidelines still apply – notices should still be dated, numbered and distributed in accordance with a pre-scheduled list of recipients, the colour coding can be utilised, and the guidelines, regarding clarity and accuracy, should be observed. As part of the management or cascade briefing system, the leader may wish to check that notices are seen and read, and possibly could refer to notices having particular relevance and importance. This is an example of the interlinking of communication methods – each has its part to play and each part can support the others.

Newspapers, newsletters, journals and magazines

The concept of producing a newspaper internal to the organisation is very widespread, and many are of a high standard and highly regarded by employees. In most organisations, around 70 per cent of staff claim to read most or all of the house paper, journal or whatever it is called. The process of generating communication via a newspaper is complex and will be dealt with in detail in Chapter 10. It is important to realise that despite the undoubted value of such a document, it can only ever support or enhance the communication process. Most newspapers are produced monthly or less frequently and thus entirely lack the immediacy of their national counterparts. Sadly, internal newspapers are often compared with the national media and criticised as such because they are not as effective. Only if an internal newspaper is produced daily will it be able to achieve the information dissemination of its national counterparts.

Case study 8.7
UNFAIR CRITICISM

The John Lewis Partnership (JLP) is actually largely owned by its employees – hence its name – and its employees are called 'partners'. Its house journal appears regularly and allows all aspects of the operation to be challenged by the partners, and, if they pose questions, requires answers to be provided by the director or manager responsible. This 'open challenge' philosophy was contrasted with a failure to provide it with a comment by a national newspaper which had picked up a story of the closure of one of the JLP stores. The company refused to comment (and was criticised by the paper for its refusal) as it wanted to speak to the staff involved first and, indeed, understandably, had wanted to keep the matter confidential until the staff who were affected had been told. Ironically, of course, simply refusing to comment was taken as an indication that the story was true.

Key technique
National newspapers work with horizons of two to three hours – far shorter than those applicable to documents produced for most other organisations, where two to three weeks (or even months) is normal. Internal communications generally, let alone an organisation's newspapers, cannot compete with that level of immediacy.

If there is information which requires immediacy of approach and response, other methods must be used – such as memos, letters, E-mail or, of course, as has been stressed repeatedly, face-to-face communication.

Memos and letters

The possibility of distributing notices instead of posting them on boards is mentioned above. This renders them somewhat akin to memos and letters, and they may suffer by being so regarded.

Providing memos are kept short, and are used for the recording of information or data, essential for the record, they have a valuable role to play as part of the communication process. Unfortunately, in some organisations, memos are used as weapons, with departments issuing them to support a stance and downface an opponent to 'prove' a particular point or to safeguard the back of the author from attack from another quarter. In such an organisation, far from being a means of communication, the memo becomes a form of red tape, the effect of which may be to block what should be open channels of communication.

To the manager with a secretary or even a word processor it seems easier to record one's thoughts, or request action by means of a memo or letter, rather than walking along the corridor or down a few stairs to discuss the matter with its intended recipient. There is, however, no substitute for face-to-face communication and save where the information is needed for the record, memos and letters which attempt to substitute for face-to-face communication should be outlawed. Not only will communication improve, but also the time and cost inherent in the production of the document, and its transportation, will be saved. Not all memos use paper. The growth of the use of answering machines internally as well as externally can lead to verbal memos being left on such machines. Unfortunately the machines are not infallible and it may be necessary to confirm the message in a written memo – this process can be fraught with problems.

103

Case study 8.8
THANKS A LOT

We refer to the above matter and are in receipt of your favoured communication of the 18th ultimo received in our office on 19th ultimo, the contents of which have been noted. In response thereof the writer left a message on your answering machine which we trust you have received.

Key technique

This really should win a prize for a most hopeless piece of communication material. Presumably it emanated from an organisation that could charge the recipient for every action. Not only does it use old English – it really is well past the time that 'ultimo' was given a (not particularly decent) burial – but also it fails to achieve what the writer wanted to achieve when he tele-phoned in the first place. It does not tell the recipient what the message was and takes a great deal of his time to do so. If the answering machine did not function properly, then the recipient is no wiser as to the message.

104   As with most such guidelines, there is an exception – and the exception to attempting to ban memos or letters concerns the handwritten format. Since most written communication is in a printed or typewrit-ten form, a handwritten memo can have a considerable appeal and impact since it indicates that 'the old man must be concerned about this (or must give this high priority) – look he's even written the note him-self'. Thus a chief executive wishing to draw a particular achievement or requirement to the attention of employees, could capture this appeal, by handwriting a few lines to the department(s) concerned. Such obviously personal attention is as valuable a communication con-duit as recognition and praise.

The advantage of memos and letters is that they do have some form of immediacy if used appropriately, and may often generate a reply which creates the communicative process. This tends to be the case only where those in receipt of a memo or letter have access to the equipment that will generate a reply – that is a typewriter or word pro-cessor. Some organisations have improved the flow of information by using self-copying memo sets, on which the recipient can insert his or her answer. Not only do both correspondents have a copy of the exchange, due to the self-copying arrangement, but also the fact that the content is very often handwritten adds to immediacy and in-formality, and creates a rapport which is very much the essence of communication.

Bulletins, fact sheets and leaflets

Although included in a resumé of communication means, these formats are essentially one-way information providers, which is not to say that their use is not important, merely to indicate that we should not expect too much of them in terms of generating rapport, commitment or communication. Basically they tend to be personal copies of what we might otherwise put on the notice board or are intended to deal with matters which would not be appropriate subjects for notice board treatment. They may also include data which might, after immediate scanning, provide back-up information and therefore require keeping.

Case study 8.9
DUAL PURPOSE

The Esso Petroleum company produces a regular *Update* for its employees and franchisees. The *Update* is essentially a journal produced to a high standard of both content and presentation. However, to the outsider its immediate appeal may be offset by the inclusion of a centre four page spread which seems to bear little direct relationship to the rest of the content. This spread is meant to be removed from the journal, and provide a source of information and data, which may mean that it is intended to be filed in a separate folder.

If such factsheets are intended to be kept to provide reference material, and/or to brief employees or provide guidance as and when the situation requires it, suitable binders should be provided and, should the number grow, a regularly updated index or contents list be provided. While not essentially communication, such items can be invaluable to employees, since they can indicate attitudes and actions required in a range of situations. They can also engender communications.

Case study 8.10
FEEDBACK

The director was extremely concerned that with over 300 outlets he was not being advised of loss causing or loss potential incidents, which might either need corrective action to avoid repetition, or be claimable under the organisation's comprehensive insurance portfolio. In addition, the organisation was endeavouring to introduce risk management principles in order to both reduce risks, and to determine how much of such risks the organisation should bear itself and how much it should pass on to its insurers.

From his regular 'walking the job' practice, he was well aware that virtually all those on whom the obligation to notify him would fall were extremely busy, with priorities that would 'outrank' his own requirements. Feeling that using his position or exhortations to let him know of all losses was not sufficient to keep the requirement in the front of such respondents' minds, he developed a process which:

- provided to the respondents regular updates (bulletins) on all aspects of the covers in force, and explained the principles that were being adopted regarding risk assessment and reduction;

- invited their suggestions that could further this process;

- encouraged their questions on and concerns about the process, which could be phoned through to him or discussed when he walked the job;

- provided them with further updates of progress, particular problems and so on, by means of further bulletins and one-off leaflets;

- provided easy-to-read procedures to be adopted in various situations;

- provided easy-to-complete and customised forms, with a stand-by answerphone service, so that if there was no time to fill in the forms the information could be phoned through;

- stressed that all that was needed from the respondents was an initial notification. Once this was accomplished further input would be generated from head office;

- provided data lists for each occurrence that provided an instant guide to what was required to complete that initial notification.

Key technique
Essentially the director sought to regard the request as it would be regarded by those from whom he required the feedback. Accordingly he made it as easy as possible for them to comply. If it comes to a choice between doing one task which is relatively straightforward and another which is not, most people will choose to do the straightforward task first most of the time.

In case study 8.10, because he took the trouble to look at the problem from the viewpoint of 'the other side' and made it easy for them to respond as he required, considerable feedback and assistance was achieved. In this way rapport was built up with 50 correspondents, which was then used for other administration tasks within the business.

Reports

The concept of using formal reports as means of communication is somewhat flawed, although they may be a valuable first step in such a process by providing initial information. Thus, in producing an employee report (that is a simplified financial statement) the aim should be only to provide information. Communication concerning the results dealt with in the report can be achieved in briefing sessions held subsequent to the receipt of the report by the target audience.

107

Feedback

As noted, one of the problems with going into print rather than carrying out face-to-face communication is that the recipient cannot ask questions of the piece of paper. Since true communication is two-way, written material on its own cannot substitute for it. Conversely there may be no other way in which, in a complex organisation or group, or one that is spread geographically, that information can be promulgated to a large number. Some means by which questions can be posed and answered must be provided. Hence, a question slip might be provided at the foot of each item with an invitation to submit the question for individual answer, or preferably more widespread answer in, for example, the company newspaper or a one-off publication. Using the newspaper answer rather than an individual response would enable anonymous questions to be answered. The manner in which the process is arranged is relatively unimportant; what is essential is that an opportunity to ask questions and receive answers is provided.

9

Clarity, clarity, clarity

'Riding on the Robert E. Lee'

Key learning points

1 The three vital (but often overlooked) ingredients of all written material are clarity, clarity and clarity.
2 To gain attention a format and presentation suitably enticing for the target audience must be chosen
3 Complex language, buzz words, jargon and the like should be avoided, and preference given to clear, concise, everyday English
4 Develop guidelines to avoid the 'permanence of print' traps.

Since it is very difficult for organisations of any size for the face-to-face process to be used by Number 1 or even other senior management in communicating with employees, most are virtually forced to use less effective written means. Using a written format provides both advantage and challenge. We have the advantage that we are able to marshal all our thoughts and views, supporting facts and data, and to present the whole in one smooth presentation, safe in the knowledge that we cannot be interrupted as we could be were we to deliver the same content verbally. All our thoughts can be expressed and we have time to give consideration to each, and to marshal our thoughts and ideas into the best order. We can propound our ideas persuasively and the challenge is to provide information in such a way that we can answer (even pre-empt) all the possible questions (and even a few impossible ones!). There is pressure to attempt this since we will not be present to gauge the views of the recipient, and to explain and help them understand our intended meaning, or to answer the questions our item generates. People are only persuaded by things that they understand and so, if we want our material to create a reaction, it is essential that it is clear, unambiguous and easy to understand.

Case study 9.1
IF IT'S GOOD ENOUGH FOR HIM . . .

The famous US General Robert E. Lee picked to be his batman a succession of men who were not particularly bright. He would seek out the slowest thinking private, even though he could have the pick of the force. When asked why, he replied that whenever he wrote out an order he would give it to his batman and ask him if he understood it. If the batman said 'No', then he would take it back and rewrite it until the batman said 'Yes'. Then Lee would ask the batman what he would do in accordance with the order. Only if the batman told him he would do what Lee wanted the recipients of the order to do, would Lee publish the order.

Key technique
By checking out receptivity and accuracy with someone of limited capacity and slow comprehension, Lee knew that his order would be clearly understood in the way he wished. If you have written something and the reader does not understand it – that is your mistake and it is your responsibility to change it. Written communication must be composed with the aim of comprehension of the target audience. If writing for those well used to handling complex written documentation, we can use complex and involved sentences, and even jargon, fairly confident that the audience will understand. If our target audience is a cross-section of employees, the language, style and layout must be suitable to their requirements – their comprehension is our responsibility.

109

The Robert E. Lee 'law of clarity' should always be remembered when we come to express ourselves in writing. In writing we lack the benefit of body language to express ourselves and provide shades of emphasis to our words. We also lack the ability to try other words in an explanatory or supplementary way if the recipient does not understand (and we will usually know they do not understand by a slightly glazed look in their eyes). We cannot recall our written words if the meaning or emphasis is wrong. To counter this our written version of what we would otherwise have 'talked' may be somewhat longer than the verbal version. This is perhaps inevitable but not necessarily disastrous. 'I am sorry this is a long letter, but I didn't have time to write a short one', said Bismarck the nineteenth-century unifier of Germany. It takes great skill to write briefly, yet coherently and comprehensively – and our first draft will rarely be our best. Indeed, as Johnson said 'what is written without effort is in general read without pleasure'. Since our aim is to ensure our words are read and understood, particularly as we are using them as a substitute for a personal presentation, we need not only to ensure we cover all the content in a way that will satisfy the abilities of Lee's batman, but also that we provide them in a format where the recipient *wants* to read them (that is they are 'pleasurable' in the widest sense of the word).

Presentation is six-sevenths of the problem

The Americans invented the Iceberg Theory which can be applied to a number of instances. Icebergs apparently float majestically on the surface of the water, whereas actually they are suspended in the water with around six-sevenths of their volume actually under the surface. Thus when we 'see' an iceberg we actually see only its visible tip. Written communication is, like the iceberg, not simply about content, though it is vital that this is accurate and comprehensive, it is to a much greater extent about presentation; about using a format which is perceived by the recipient to be user-friendly so that it entices their initial attention and then retains that attention so that they read the whole. When we write we should really consider 'designing' the piece of writing, considering from the start how it will appear on the page, how it can capture attention and how it can retain attention.

Literacy problems

It is not as though all our audience are likely to be waiting for our every word with bated breath. In the UK:

- 50 per cent of the population does not buy a book from one end of the year to the other;
- one in seven of school leavers admit to having difficulty with reading; and
- 8,000,000 have such low literacy skills they may be unable to follow up a job advert.

(Source: *Sunday Times*/WH Smith 'Wordpower', 1992).

In addition, it is estimated that between 2 and 4 per cent of the UK population suffer from dyslexia, which further impairs the reading ability of target audiences. Most of those with less than average reading ability (other, presumably, than the 300,000 who cannot read at all) do regularly read, or at least scan, a national newspaper. In the UK we have a range of newspapers which, in terms of wordiness or presentation, range from the 'wordy', 'heavy' or 'quality', *Times, Independent* and *Guardian*, to the 'picture/headline orientated' 'light', tabloids like the *Sun* and the *Mirror*, with titles like the *Telegraph, Express* and *Mail* somewhere between the two extremes. The readership tends to shrink as one passes from the 'light tabloid' to the 'heavy quality' titles, which indicates that in the average workforce a fair proportion will be used to receiving their written material presented with pictorial support and 'copy signposts', that is using bold headlines, subheadings and extended captions.

While not advocating that an organisation's communication material needs to be presented as the tabloids present their copy, there is no doubt that if we wish to present written material in a style which approaches theirs, we need to consider such presentation carefully. With national papers, readers have a choice and can match their requirements to the paper that most closely satisfies them. With in-company material they have no such choice. Present data in the form and style used by *The Times* to someone used to reading the *Sun*, will assure only inattention. It is normally argued that a style near that of the *Daily Mail* should be acceptable to most people in most audiences.

111

'Fine words butter no parsnips'

By this phrase (from 'The Legend of Montrose') Sir Walter Scott meant that it is possible to use language which may have no practical use, although it reflects well on the speaker. Thus, the actual language we use may itself pose barriers to comprehension. Sadly there are many who feel that only if they use high-flown language, complex sentences, buzz words and all the rest of what can be described as a kind of literary smokescreen, will their written material be 'effective'. In fact, only if the whole lot is junked and instead ordinary, everyday English is employed, will it have the slightest chance of working with the average target audience.

112

In the novel *1984*, George Orwell invented the land of totalitarianism ruled by Big Brother where to try to contain or remove dissident thought, the language, 'Newspeak', was reduced to very few words. While as far as its actual intent goes, such a concept is impossible, the theory of using fewer rather than more words is sound. Away from the nightmarish *1984*, Orwell developed a number of guidelines for the good use of English, including those set out below.

Guidelines to written language

- Avoid using a metaphor or simile, or other figure of speech which you are used to seeing in print.

- Use short words rather than long words.

- Avoid verbosity – cut out redundant words.

- Never use jargon, or scientific or foreign words, if you can use ordinary, everyday English words.

- Always use the active tense rather than the passive and, above all,

- break any or all of these guidelines rather than say anything that is outright barbarous!

From *Politics and the English Language* by George Orwell

Once we deviate from guidelines like these, we can become trapped in a 'Newspeak' of our own, where the words constantly get in the way of the meaning.

> **Case study 9.3**
> **'I'M SORRY, I'LL READ THAT AGAIN'**
>
> 113
>
> This specially produced guide will immediately furnish YOU, the purchaser, with a comprehensive and in-depth guide to the operation, capability and accessibility of this Super Widget.
>
> Minus all the gobbledegook this sentence actually says 'This tells you how it works', which could be further shortened to the simple headline: 'How it works'.

Watch out – there's a thief about

The thief in this case has, as his target, clarity. It is all too easy to adopt the habit of using phrases, jargon and 'in-words'. Jargon, when used in material intended for some who will be unfamiliar with it, can be said to be the refuge of the insecure, an excuse for the lazy and the language of the patronising. The perpetrators are:

- insecure in that they may be attempting to protect their position by surrounding it with terminology which only the 'privileged few' can understand;

- lazy since they cannot be bothered to explain the true meaning of the jargon to ensure clarity and comprehension;

- patronising their reader by inferring that if 'you don't understand the jargon, why are you bothering to read this at all?'

114

Case study 9.4
'SORRY?'

The UK recession has been a period of retrenchment, reassessment and restructuring for most of the operators who find themselves in our industry. We have not sought to exclude ourselves from this general trend and have taken active steps to preserve competitiveness and market share, despite considerable external pressures. We are in the process of carrying out a comprehensive appraisal of the long term profitability of each of our operating divisions which is leading to the termination of some products past their peak selling capacity and this in turn is leading to a requirement for an overhaul of our staffing capacity and the assessment of the proper utilisation of group assets.

Phew! This is a model example of how the use of jargon and high-flown corporate phrases simply ensures that the average reader cannot really comprehend the message that those astute or experienced enough to read between the lines can discern. Basically the message is:

We've had a tough time, which is likely to continue, and to react to the new market conditions, staff and assets surplus to current requirements will be dispensed with.

Expressed in that ordinary language, most people in the country, let alone the company, should be able to understand its message. They might not like it, but dressing bad news up in gobbledegook doesn't make it any more palatable. Indeed, it may so aggravate the reader when the message is translated into everyday English for them, their understandable response may be 'Why the hell didn't you say so in the first place?'

Key technique
Patronising the reader leading to their aggravation is the swiftest route to losing the very rapport that the communication process is trying to achieve.

Case study 9.5
'WHAT WAS THAT AGAIN?'

All the players in the local economy recognise that the prognosis is bleak, that complacency is unwarranted and that greater more proactive public sector leverage is required if the local community is to realise the area's economic potential.

Key technique
Hopefully the author knows what he or she means, but I doubt if many readers do and, if not, what has been the point of using such complex language? It will merely irritate those who bother to read past the first few words.

Fog

115

Using long, complex and unwieldy language creates uncertainty where what was attempted was clarity. The more complex and obtuse the language, the higher the 'fog factor'. In preparing items, particularly for a written format, although to some extent the same principle applies to verbal presentations, fog needs to be guarded against.

Count the number of words (at least 100) in a piece of prose. Divide that number by the number of sentences. Count two or more complete thoughts separated by a comma, colon or semi-colon in one longer sentence as a separate sentence. This gives you the average sentence length.

Count the number of words with three or more syllables. Ignore for this purpose words which are made up of shorter words such as 'caretaker'. Divide the multisyllable words by the word total and multiply by 100. Add the average sentence length to the multisyllable percentage figure. Multiply the result by 0.4. The result is the fog index for that piece of writing.

In the above definition are 112 words and 10 sentences. Average sentence length = 11.2.

There are 12 words with three or more syllables giving a multisyllable percentage of (12/112 x 100) which is 10.7.

Adding 11.2 and 10.7 we obtain 21.9 which multiplied by 0.4 results in 8.76. The nearer to 0 the result is, the less fog there is.

The same definition could be written by fog devotees as follows:

To arrive at the calculation of the fog index one has to take several steps commencing with counting the number of words (totalling at least 100) in the selected piece of writing. Following that the investigator is required to count the number of sentences including for this purpose as whole sentences disparate parts of a sentence separated by punctuation marks such as a comma or a colon. The number of words must then be divided by the number of 'sentences' to calculate the average length of each such sentence.

The next step is to count the number of words of or exceeding three syllables, excluding those comprising two or more smaller words such as 'caretaker', and divide the number of multisyllable words by the total number of words already discovered, and add the result to the average sentence length and multiply by 0.4 in order to discover the fog index for that composition.

This time we find: words – 153, sentences – 7. Average sentence length: 21.8.

Multisyllable words: 22   Percentage of total words: 14.4.

Total 36.2 x 0.4 = 14.48, which is approaching a veritable pea-souper!

The 12 Commandments

So widely are the written means of communication used, and often with so little thought, it may be helpful to reduce the advice regarding the preparation of written copy to the 12 practical hints set out below.

1 Remember KISS. KISS in this context stands for 'keep it short and simple'. An alternative version runs 'keep it simple, stupid', and the same mnemonic (or at least one that runs KISSSSSS) can be also made to stand for 'keep it:

- simple
- sharp
- short
- slim

- straightforward and
- suitable!'

You may be criticised by some but at least you should be understood by all. Written material does not necessarily become easier to understand if it is made longer. Indeed, research indicates that on average attention to and retention by the target audience decreases in direct proportion to the length of the content. A message, article or report on a single sheet of paper is far more likely to attain and retain attention than an item several times its size. Indeed, it is not unknown for recipients to read only the first and last page of bulky items. Similarly, even with items for which a charge has been made (for example, newspapers) rarely is every word read. The tendency is to skim rather than to read. The shorter the item, and the more 'user-friendly' the way in which it is presented, the more likely it is that the piece will be read with attention.

117

Case study 9.6
FEW QUESTIONED THOSE FIGURES

In the mid 1970s a president of a large American corporation, wishing to check how much of the data contained in management reports were actually studied, stapled the centrefold of the current edition of *Playboy* into a report and sent it out on a 'Read, initial and pass on' circulation to a set of named managers. Out of the ten who received and passed it on, only two subsequently queried with him why, amidst its data, were other, perhaps more attractive, statistics on display.

Key technique
If wishing to ensure that at least the aims and recommendations of the material/report are read, set these out on both the first and the last page of the item. The data, background information and so on, should be in the middle. Above all, however, try to restrict the length, if necessary leaving out the data and simply stating its availability for those who wish to refer to it, so that the recommendations stand out clearly.

---

2 Make the content enticing – use headlines and other 'text signposts' to avoid the reader's eye being repelled by masses of uninviting text.

3 Decide on the message, write that message and then check what you have written conveys your original intended message. If it does, use it, if not remember why General Lee chose his batman.

4 Keep the target audience and their requirements in mind. If they are college professors or lawyers they should be able to handle complex written material and indeed may prefer their data presented in this way. It is unlikely whether the same is true of the average employee. The content must be user-friendly and user-aimed.

Case study 9.7
WE ARE NOT AMUSED

The UK prime minister has a regular (usually weekly) audience with the monarch. This custom started during the reign of Queen Victoria. Her preference for the procedure was offset, however, when William Gladstone became prime minister. 'He speaks to me as if I were a public meeting' she complained to a courtier.

Key technique
The content and the presentation must be appropriate to the circumstances and also to the target audience.

---

5 Use short sentences. Complex sentences tend to confuse the average reader. If the reader has to reread the sentence to try and understand the meaning, first it means that the writer has failed, and secondly, it may irritate the reader so much that their attention is lost both to that sentence and to the rest of the item. Short sentences are also very effective when trying to make important points.

6 Don't become trapped into overusing the same words – particularly verbs.

Case study 9.8
GOT TO GET RID OF GET

Getting up, he got his book from the shelf, went outside and got into his car and went to the library. He got out, got a free paper from the bin by the library and went into the building. He got some new books out, got back into his car and went home. He got it all done in 19 minutes.

> **Key technique**
> *It may be simple and certainly clear but it is also boring even though the aim of the author was to try and give the impression of speed. However, there are other ways of doing this – what we must do is consider the language we use. Thus, an alternative version could read:*
>
> > *In a rush to borrow some titles before the library closed, he swiftly drove himself into town, grabbing a free paper on the way. Not bothering to spend too much time on his selection of books he was back home in less than 20 minutes.*

7 Don't link dissimilar ideas – apart from the fact that they will tend to make the sentence overlong, the dissimilarity of the content can confuse.

8 Avoid using nouns as verbs. Verbs are the 'doing' words and should be used in that context. 'After lunch we will car the group to Factory X' may be shorter than 'After lunch the group will be taken by car to Factory X', but the latter is unlikely to be misunderstood, while the former makes the reader wonder if the typist meant to insert 'carry' which then makes the wording so fascinating that the required attention to the message may be lost! Remember 'If it is extremely interesting, it is almost certainly wrong'.

9 Don't use jargon (unless the only readers are those familiar with its use and you can be confident everyone understands it clearly) or prefabricated phrases. For example, phrases such as 'significant progress has been achieved' are imprecise unless supported by data. What may be significant to one may be insignificant to another. 'Our decisions have been set in the context of a strategic incorporated plan with goals, targets and mission statements' was an example quoted by Secretary of State for Wales John Redwood, as part of a plea for managers to speak and use everyday English. He commented that with this kind of language one 'was left wondering whether you are playing football, practising archery or have perhaps landed on the moon'. It may be preferable to include facts and exclude comment, although this will depend on the context of the item.

119

10 Avoid prefabricated phrases, buzz words or the definitions beloved of the political correctness movement. 'With this mechanical explosive device I am creating a hostile environment for the frequency distribution of feathered edible aerofoils' may sound very grand but actually all it means is 'I am shooting ducks'. 'Vertically challenged' apparently means 'short' but as a short person I find it patronising. I can also challenge it since it infers that it is 'right' to be tall, whereas I could argue it is tall people who are vertically challenged since it is 'right' to be short! Similarly a 'woman' is now defined as 'a person of gender' – but surely so is a man? The effect of using such phrases and words is merely to baffle and irritate the reader. The effect of such irritation is to impair the acceptance of the message.

11 Avoid using 'flannel' or 'hype'. 'Flannel' means using phrases and language which say little but try to cover up the reality, whereas 'hype' is short for hyperbole which means 'a phrase which is exaggerated but not meant to be taken seriously'. While this may be of use in some contexts beware the indiscriminate use of such patronising tactics, which may aggravate some readers or listeners and, once again, impair the message.

The idea of sincerely meant congratulations is fine – the language is 'OTT' (over the top), particularly as in this instance the workforce knew, though apparently the chairman did not, that the order had been filed instead of being scheduled for production, and that it was only by luck the mistake had been discovered. In order to meet the delivery deadline, and thanks to some inept industrial relations on the part of Joe Bloggs, the union had held out for, and won, an additional bonus for those working on the order, who had finished up working for nearly 24 hours on a rate in excess of double time. Irrespective of the fine words, the workforce knew the truth: 'efficient and economic' working it certainly was not, while the general opinion was that Joe should have been fired rather than applauded.

Key technique
Employees are not fools, and using hype and exaggeration can destroy credibility and rapport, when considerably at variance with the facts. Such wording might be acceptable in an external document, since employees will understand the need to present an efficient face to the world, and may often themselves defend externally what privately they may criticise strenuously.

121

12 Don't try to rewrite history. In writing for external publication most authors will wish to show the organisation in a good light, a situation which most employees will appreciate. However, in writing communication material for internal consumption, such revised versions are (like hype) unacceptable. Truth, honesty and consistency are needed.

Case study 9.11
ORWELL WOULD BE PROUD OF YOU, SIR

In *1984*, whenever there was a subsequent occurrence which showed previous comments or actions by Big Brother in a poor light, the solution was simple: history was simply rewritten so that Big Brother could be shown to have been right all along.

The organisation had been through a difficult period and communications had suffered, although the employees had a fairly clear idea of each development – and memories to match. The board, however, had been trying to present each development to the outside world as if it had been thought out in advance.

Employees will be pleased to learn that in accordance with previous indications of our strategy, we have decided to withdraw from the

> Bloggs business and to concentrate our efforts on our core businesses. We will be converting the assets currently used in the Bloggs business into income-earning entities mainly on a leased basis to outsiders.
>
> The employees could easily remember that the two previous announcements referred to investment in the Bloggs business and the fact that a better return was anticipated from that business than by using assets elsewhere.
>
> *Key technique*
> *Employees are not fools and can understand that changes of direction need to be taken – often for good reasons. It would be far more effective to explain the reasons for the change of direction, rather than trying to convince everyone that history did not happen the way everyone remembers it.*

In case study 9.11, if instead of going into print, matters had been dealt with in a verbal presentation, the board might have got away with it. But once the items are in print there will always be at least one copy to give the lie to the statement. Losing credibility on a matter like this raises questions of credibility on all other items, as well as undermining the basis of the communication exercise.

10

Publishing internally

'Mentioned in dispatches'

Key learning points

1 Internal newspapers or journals can provide links with and, provided they are encouraged to contribute, engender feedback from employees
2 Newspapers must be well prepared and executed, with business news restricted to no more than 25 per cent
3 Writers must present their material in ways which entice and retain attention
4 The interests of the target audience must always be in the forefront of the minds of authors – clarity must be the watchword.

The visual image society

The greatest communication force in our modern western world is television. Very few are not subjected to the images it creates daily, even though comprehensive television coverage is not much more than one generation old.

Our ancestors who fought with Henry V lived in a verbal world. Such books as there were, were of use to only a very restricted few. The power of story-telling and rumour was immense – but the images they created were in the head of the listener.

With the development of mechanised printing, our great grandparents found a world where the written word became increasingly powerful – thus the newspaper *The Times* was known as 'the Thunderer' since it was a powerful opinion maker. Essentially images were still in the mind of the reader – there were few illustrations other than cartoons.

Our grandparents lived in a world which had partly reverted to verbal power with the invention of radio. However, improvements in printing processes meant that the printed word could still hold its own since only newspapers and journals could present visual images of stories recounted on the 'wireless'.

Nowadays, for most people, television has overtaken all other media as a purveyor of instant news reports. Unlike all other media, however, it tends to reverse the usual method of presentation – first find the story, then find the illustration. The nature of the medium requires that the picture is all-important. It is vital to remember this, since if we want our readers to read what we have provided and more important to respond, we need to present our written information in a visually appealing way since that is the way most people normally receive such information.

Aping the outside world

With the above in mind one of the most effective means of mass information within an organisation is the production of a regular newspaper, newsletter or journal. The most successful of these swiftly become a part of the life of the organisation and can contribute in a considerable way to the dissemination of information, as well as encouraging a two-way dialogue – that is communication. A newspaper should never be or become a management mouthpiece, but it is quite legitimate to use it as a tool for dissemination. The overriding consideration in producing a newspaper is that it should be fun or, at the very least, enjoyable. It should be enjoyable to read, enjoyable to write for, enjoyable to edit and an enjoyable contribution to organisation life. This does not mean it should trivialise its content, but there is no doubt that unless it is presented with lightness and life it will not entice readership, and thus will not be read.

Name

The newspaper needs a good attractive name which should be:

- related to the organisation;
- short and catchy;
- an attention grabber;
- instantly recognisable.

The name itself should virtually become a brand – being promoted by and promoting the newspaper in turn.

Case study 10.1
EH?

Xerox Corporation's publishing interests in Europe and Africa were described as being in the 'Eastern Hemisphere' and the initials of those words formed part of the title of that part of its group – Xerox Publishing Group (EH). When the UK companies wished to start a company newsletter they chose the title *'EH?'* echoing the initials contained in part of the group's name but also symbolising an awakening of interest.

Key technique
While 'Bloggs News' may be an intended description of the publication, this may promote the concept that its content is (only) organisation oriented. In addition, the name needs to address the frequency of its publication. 'XYZ News' is hardly appropriate for a quarterly publication as, by the time each issue appears, much of its content may be stale – hardly 'news' at all. Obviously 'Bloggs Old Hat items' is hardly appropriate, but 'Bloggs Update' or 'Bloggs Reporter' may be.

125

A 'good' newspaper

While an organisation newspaper cannot provide all the answers if there are communication problems, there is no doubt that it can help 'bridge the gap'. MORI found that over 70 per cent of the average workforce tend to read most of their in-house newspaper and many publications score even more highly. So what is it that makes a good in-house newspaper? Research in the 1980s indicated that the 'best' in-house papers (that is the most successful in terms of readership acceptability) were those which had the following characteristics:

- encouraged employees to contribute;
- restricted business news to 25 per cent of total;
- featured general interest stories;
- controlled the item internally; and
- had a perceived and appropriate value/quality.

Of these the most important characteristic is undoubtedly encouraging employees to contribute. If they do, they are endorsing the way it is produced, claiming some proprietorial interest in it, encouraging their colleagues to read and write for it, and generating two-way communication.

The editor

When introducing a newspaper these factors should be borne in mind and form part of the brief to the editor. The editor is critical to the publication, as are the terms under which he or she should operate. Ideally the editor should be someone with senior management status or, at least, if not of such status, someone who has instant access to top management for quotes, guidance and input. This is not a question of censorship, which should be avoided, but merely a matter of being aware of the realities of the situation. The editor may not be privy to decisions made by the board, but should be guided to avoid situations where susceptibilities can be harmed.

Case study 10.2
IN THE NICK OF TIME

The editor was delighted – she had a good quality action photo of several employees thoroughly enjoying themselves at a social event, and she had written an equally bright and breezy story relating their leisure time activities to working efficiently. She was about to use the story and the photo on the front page of the next issue of the journal when her director happened to see it and stopped the process. He explained that redundancies were about to be announced at that factory and most of those in the photo would be affected.

Key technique
While not advocating censorship in any way (since if the readership becomes aware that the organisation is censoring items, their regard for it will fall and they will be less likely to contribute), to avoid potential backlashes, some kind of top management overview may be required.

To try to avoid problems and provide guidance for the editor a brief such as the example set out below should be drawn up, while its publication should be referred to within the communication policy.

1 The Journal will be entitled .... and will be edited by .... It will be produced .... times each year on .... (publication dates) ....

2 Its purposes are to

(a) provide a communication channel between company and employees, employees and company, and employees and employee (employees in this context include active and retired personnel, and their relatives and dependants)

(b) provide information on company, personnel and personal activities, product sales and launches performance, industry activities and so on

(c) provide information on and comprehension of the financial results of the company

(d) help create a rapport among those working in and concerned with the company

(e) help improve the commitment of the employees to the aims of the company.

3 It will be produced primarily for the active employees of the company but should also seek to satisfy the requirements of retired employees, shareholders who have requested they be placed on the mailing list, company suppliers and customers.

4 It should be realised that it is possible the Journal could be read by competitors and for this reason discretion should be exercised when featuring reports on new products, financial results, processes etc.

5 Since the Journal will be read outside the company – even if this may not be the intent – it is expected that its presentation, style and content should be of such a standard that it will not detract from the reputation or standing of the company.

6 The Board does not wish there to be any censorship of items included, but does expect the Editor to try to maintain an acceptable standard of English and content, and to avoid giving offence to any reader or section of readers, in keeping with the existing ethos of the company.

7 The Journal may deal with all matters arising from the activities of the company, except those relating to an individual's pay and/or benefits, contract terms, personal details and/or life unless he/she has so authorised in writing in advance.

8 The Editor and the Journal will be bound by the confidential agreement applicable to all Directors and Staff regarding the issue and use of price-sensitive information.

9 The Journal should avoid making criticisms of any internal or external person or body, unless that body is given a right of reply. Any such reply should appear adjacent to the criticisms, in the same issue, and enjoy commensurate space and position. Anonymous letters or articles [MAY BE/ARE NOT] to be featured.

10 If the Editor is unsure whether to include a particular article he/she should refer to .... for guidance.

11 The Editor will have complete discretion (subject to this Statement) regarding content and presentation but will endeavour at all times to ensure the Journal satisfies its aims as set out above, particularly (d) and (e).

12 The Editor will be responsible for compiling and submitting a budget to the .... and for adhering to that budget. Special features such as the History of the Company and the celebration of the company's seventy-fifth anniversary which are to be featured in the Journal will be subject to a supplementary budget to be agreed separately.

13 The budget will need to reflect external sourcing of all design, illustrating and printing facilities. The Editor will have the use of word processing facilities in the .... dept.

128

Although one person in sole charge is possibly preferable to an editorial committee, this should not mean the editor should be the only writer. All management and employees should be encouraged to write. This can be by general invite, although to provide encouragement, or to help logistics with a geographically spread group, the editor may wish to 'appoint' local correspondents to write regularly and/or to encourage others located near them to write.

Making writers of readers

If the newspaper is intended to work as a two-way communication tool, this will only occur if the editor encourages as many employees as possible to contribute. While this can give rise to problems of content and quality, care must be taken not to discourage any reader from becoming a writer as the more employees who can be encouraged to write for the newspaper, the more proprietorial will be their attitude, and the greater will be their commitment to the paper and its sponsoring organisation.

Case study 10.3
SHOT IN THE FOOT

The director had written about 85 per cent of the first issue of the new company journal and was very pleased with the end result. It was dispatched to all parts of the group with personal invitations to all employees to contribute to the next and subsequent issues. However, when such material was received, the editor was concerned at its relatively poor quality. Feeling inhibited about altering it so that an 'acceptable' quality was achieved, he discarded it. It then became difficult to generate more items as readers were aware that some 'quality censorship' had been at work. It took a year to recover the impetus so thoughtlessly stopped.

Key technique
If copy is inadequate either:

1 *rewrite it under a heading 'From Joe Bloggs we hear that ...' using some of the original wording duly corrected;*

2 *rewrite it as part of another article with similar interest; or*

3 *telephone or interview the author and gather some more information, and then write a story featuring quotes as well as some of the original copy duly 'improved'.*

In fact most correspondents submitting poorly constructed articles expect the editor to correct spelling and grammar, and are in no way insulted when this occurs.

129

To try to ensure as much copy as possible is provided as near to the quality required a correspondents' brief, like the one below, may be useful.

SUBMITTING ITEMS

1 Copy for [News] is required by the copy dates which are [dates].

2 Copy is ideally submitted typed double-spaced (that is written on every other line) on one side of A4 paper, but handwritten copy will be accepted provided it is clearly written (again double-spaced and on one side of the paper). There is no need to worry about grammar and spelling as this can be automatically corrected at the editing stage of production.

Accuracy

3 Authors should try at all times to be accurate and to provide full details of all items included in the copy. For example, dates, places, names (fore-names and surnames), locations, departments etc., should be included (in capitals, if the copy is handwritten, to avoid misunderstandings of spellings).

Wordage

4 Other than articles written purely on an 'on spec' basis the Editor will normally indicate the number of words required. It can be difficult to write to a set number of words but every effort should be made to keep to any wordage required as this indicates that space has been allocated for the article. Articles submitted which exceed the number of words required will need to be edited.

Title and headings

5 The article should bear a suitable title although the editor reserves the right to change this or to substitute another.

6 The style of [News] is such that we require bite-sized pieces of text. Articles should be broken up into paragraphs of no more than [number of words – this will depend on the type of layout, number of columns etc.], with each introduced by a heading, quotation or wording which either leads into the following paragraph or indicates its content.

Style

7 Our style is relaxed and articles should be written in this way. Try to avoid using jargon or, if it is inevitable, explain it. Try to vary the words used – especially verbs – as this will aid the attractiveness of the piece. However, don't use unusual words just for the sake of it.

Illustrations

8 All articles make a greater impact if they are supported by an illustration (photo, drawing, cartoon etc.). In writing your article try to think of suitable illustrations that could form part of the finished item. If you can source your own illustration please send it with the article – it can be returned provided a self-addressed envelope is included. A note of the name and address of the sender should be attached to the photo using detachable stickers. The rear of a photo should not be written upon.

9 Ideally photos should be taken using black and white film, and should feature action rather than posed subjects. If posed subjects must be taken, try to avoid straight lines – if there are several people site them on different levels, for example, on a staircase, or some sitting and some standing, etc. If possible take three or four shots of the same subject from different angles and send them all in.

Usage

10 Copy and illustrations are submitted to the editor on the understanding that this is a voluntary and unpaid system, and that the item is the work of the person submitting the copy. If this is not the case it should be made clear on the item and, if appropriate, the agreement of the author obtained to the inclusion of the item. No guarantee of inclusion can be given either for the issue for which the item is submitted or for any subsequent issues for which it may be held over.

Correspondents

11 The correspondents acting for the Editor are as follows: (names and departments) and they will act as postboxes and immediate assistance. To save time the correspondents may check copy for completeness as it is handed in, and may request further information in order to ensure the article is complete before passing it to the editor.

Complaints

12 In the event of a complaint being made, the person or organisation against whom the complaint is made will always be given a right of reply in the same issue as the complaint appears. This may mean delaying inclusion pending receipt of the reply.

Editor's decision

13 The editor's decision regarding inclusion and/or editing of any article will be final, and no correspondence regarding such decisions can be entered into.

(Note the emphasis placed on the need for visual images – title, headlines, illustrations etc. in this brief. Essentially, as highlighted in Chapter 9, unless articles are presented in a 'user-friendly' manner – that is they are visually appealing – they may not command attention.)

To encourage/remind everyone to write for the newspaper, blank pads, bearing the newspaper's name, can be provided at each location. If these bear the editor's name and the address to which articles must be sent, while the copy dates are regularly published, there should be no excuse for contributors not to have available all the means to contribute! Every issue should bear the copy date of the next following issue, as well as an invitation to submit items with a note of the address to which they should be sent.

Top level commitment

As in all communication matters top level commitment is essential for the newspaper. If Number 1 regularly writes for the newspaper (and that means a specially written article, rather than a reprint of a message used elsewhere) then credence will be given to the newspaper, as well as communication between top floor and shop floor being encouraged. Some journals adopt an 'open forum' attitude whereby employees can ask questions, even anonymously, of management and the latter are required to reply.

132

Case study 10.4
OPEN HOUSE

The John Lewis Partnership journal *Gazette*, which recently won the Campaign for Freedom of Information's award for promoting 'free and open debate about both policy and personnel issues of a kind that most companies go out of their way to prevent' was set up by the founder of the partnership in 1918 to improve internal communication. Lewis felt that people should know what was happening in their business, and one of the features of the *Gazette* is that anyone can send in a question and management must provide an answer. Each year over 700 letters are received and all but a very small number are answered. The director of personnel regards the letters page, irritating though it may be at times, as a 'crucial element in management accountability'.

Key technique
The fact that the Partnership employees have an outlet for, and can obtain an answer about what can be their most deeply held grievances, at least means their concerns can be aired. If the concern is not aired then it cannot be dealt with and may fester. Festering concerns will always mitigate against the success of communication and help destroy motivation.

Production – general rules

The actual production of a newspaper is outside the scope of this book, but, since some of the factors that apply to the presentation of newspapers also apply to most other items of written material some general rules may be of assistance. Presenting written material for others is an art and one that is not as widely understood as it should be by many whose responsibility it is. Readers tend to 'see' (that is gain an immediate impression of) a page or double page as a composite 'picture', comprising headlines, words and illustrations. Thus the layout is important as a picture in its own right and, whether it be for a newspaper or for a report, or simply for an information document, we must design each page with this idea in mind – a meld of readable copy, headlines and illustrations. The art of the headline is not only to capture attention, but also to give a clue as to the content of the article – in short to entice the reader to pursue the interest thus generated by the instant guide. In no way should a newspaper, or any other piece of communication material, be dominated by headlines but they should certainly act as signposts.

133

In Figures 10.1 and 10.2, two pieces of copy have been reproduced. They contain virtually the same information and yet the average reader's instant reaction on being presented with them will be completely different. Slabs of text, such as that shown in Figure 10.1 will instantly repel most readers. In lecturing at locations throughout the UK during 1994, I showed these examples to around 500 delegates and asked how many would bother to read them. Only four (that is less than 1 per cent) said they would read the copy set out in Figure 10.1 although virtually everyone said they would read the copy were it presented to them as set out in Figure 10.2.

Dealing with text slabs

The problem with the copy in Figure 10.1 is primarily that it is presented in a slab of text without attention 'grabbers' or 'information pointers', in other words the content is said to be not *accessible* (which is jargon for 'can be easily accepted by the reader'). A more fundamental point, however, is that it breaks the rule that no line of type should contain more than 2.5 alphabets, that is 65 characters. Most eyes cannot cope with lines of such length, they tend to wander above and below the 'target' line. In presenting information to readers any barriers to their task need to be removed. Far too often text is presented to

CREATIVE & LEISURE STUDIES FACULTY   No 4
SPRING NEWSLETTER

Dear Parents and Pupils,
                           In another packed term of events,the Christmas Term saw many of
our pupils representing   either on the sports fields,concert platform or stage.A
number of senior pupils from the School also visited the Lucien Freud Exhibition at the
White Chapel Art Gallery as part of their project on 'figures'.
     The visit is part of the Art Department's policy of bringing students into direct contact
with the work of contemporary artists.Another exhibition that received visits from both
students and staff was that of our last Artist in Residence,Ludvic Boden.The exhibition at the
Waltham Abbey Museum was extremely successful and showed the recent work which he had
created at   ..His sculptures are witty and highly skilled,and the School was extremely
fortunate to have had this talented artist to inspire the pupil's work.The Art Department at
            is always an exciting place to visit and any parent visiting the School should pop
their heads in and admire the tremendous work our pupils produce there.Next term we will
have to cope without our Head of Art,Mrs Turner,as she starts maternity leave in May.We all
wish her well and news of the new arrival will be published in the Summer Newsletter.We are
also happy to announce that we have secured the services of two very talented and experienced
Art teachers to cover Mrs Turner's absence.
                 Last Term the Music Department presented three concerts,two at the School and one
at   Church.The first of these was a 'Recital Evening' in the Drama Studio.This was
an opportunity for the G.C.S.E Music students to develop their performance skills prior to
their examination..It was,as intended,a thoroughly enjoyable,informal and intimate evening for
all who attended.There were some excellent individual performances and a wide variety of
music on offer.Less than a month later the Department staged a large scale concert in the Main
Hall.This was the first time for several years that the Music and P.E. Departments decided that
they had enough material to fill two seperate concert programmes at Christmas,and reflects the
healthy state of music and dance in the School.The Christmas Music Concert was a sell out and
the capacity audience enjoyed a feast of seasonal music.Within a week our musicians were
tuning up again,this time to present the musical parts of the   Carol Service at
            Church.In just over a week thirty eight of our musicians will be sailing over to the
continent on a tour to Boppard on the River Rhine.It certainly is a busy time in the Music
Department,there are rehearsals every lunchtime and after school on Fridays,and we are always
grateful to our core of musicians who turn up day in and day out for rehearsals no matter what
the weather.Despite the additional hours Mr.Tubb our Head of Music has put in,he has still
found time for some courting and we were delighted when he and Miss Godfrey,the Head of
Girls P.E. announced their engagement after the half term break.
     ∪ It is a double celebration for Miss Godfrey who has recently secured the post of Head of
P.E. at Woodside school in , ~ ~   We all wish her the very best of luck in the
future,although we will miss her unbounded enthusiasm and energy tremendously.Miss
Godfrey has been at the heart of the life of   School for five years and has provided
great encouragement for many pupils particularly in trampolining and dance.She has also been
a very active member of the Staffroom Committee arranging events such as last terms staff
Quasar and bowls evening at Romford.
     ∪ Miss Godfrey's replacement will join a very active department, Mr Pepper and Miss
Templeton have provided tremendous support for Mr Huizar and the extra curricular
programme has been extended again this year.In last term's soccer season we managed to
significantly reduce the School's P.E. transport costs by departing from the County Cup
competition in the first round in all five years!We can only improve next season.At
rugby,however,we have been more successful and the Yr 7 team in particular finished in
credit.Congratulations go to Ian Peermamode in Yr 10 who has regularly played for Essex this
year as prop.Our netball team has enjoyed mixed fortunes this year with some good wins
against King Harold and Burnt Mill but defeats at the hands of Roding Valley and St.Mark's.

Figure 10.1

CREATIVE & LEISURE STUDIES FACULTY SPRING NEWSLETTER

A PACKED CHRISTMAS TERM!

Last term saw many school pupils representing ... on the sports field, on the concert platform or on stage.

ART

Several senior pupils visited the Lucien Freud exhibition at the White Chapel Art Gallery as part of their project on 'figures' and in order to bring them into contact with the work of contemporary artists.

Several pupils and staff also visited the highly successful exhibition of the work of our Artist in residence, Ludvic Boden, at Waltham Abbey Museum. Ludvic's sculpture works are witty and highly skilled and we were extremely fortunate to have had this talented artist to inspire our pupils. ...art department is always an exciting place to visit and all visitors are very welcome.

Staff changes

We look forward to welcoming two talented and experienced teachers, covering for Mrs Turner, Head of Art, during her maternity leave starting in May. We send Mrs Turner our best wishes and hope to announce the new arrival in the summer newsletter.

MUSIC

The Music department presented three concerts during last term. An informal and intimate recital evening, held in the Drama Studio provided a chance for our GCSE students to develop their performance skills before their examination.

Concert

Within a month, the Music dept., staged a large scale concert in the main Hall. For the first time for several years the Music and PE departments decided to offer separate concert programmes, evidencing the healthy state of music and dance at the School. The Christmas music concert was sold out and a capacity audience thoroughly enjoyed the feast of seasonal music.

International profile

Within a week of the concert, our musicians were tuning up again, this time playing in the Carol service at ... Church, whilst shortly 38 pupils are to leave for a tour to Boppard on the River Rhine!

Commitment

It is certainly a busy time in the music department – there are rehearsals every lunchtime and after school every Friday. We are very grateful to all those who attend so regularly.

Music department wedding bells

Despite the additional hours he gives to the department, our Head of Music, Mr Tubb recently announced his engagement to Miss Godfrey, Head of Girls PE and we send our congratulations. In fact it is a double celebration for Miss Godfrey who will shortly be leaving St Johns to take up the post of Head of PE at Woodside School. We wish her every success in the future although we will miss her unbounded enthusiasm and energy.

Figure 10.2

the reader with insufficient appreciation of how repelling some readers find slabs of grey copy – the greyness being derived from the interaction of black type on white paper. Generally, text should be broken up into digestible slabs and, if it is, will tend to be read by more of the target audience. When preparing material for employees, some of whom may find difficulty with reading substantial amounts of text, it *must* be broken up to ensure they are enticed to it and subsequently their attention is retained. Headlines are essential to grab the reader's attention, and additional 'signposts' are essential throughout the article, to hold and retain that attention, and avoid readers skimming – or simply passing on.

Many organisations have a style which they prefer to be used in all cases. Normally any such 'style guide' should be followed by the newspaper. However, where the preference is for double-justification, that is both the left and right sides of the copy are aligned (as is this text), this tends to give communication material (and especially newspapers) a somewhat formal appearance. Double justification, other than where narrow columns are used (as is the case in the national press) may be better avoided in internal communications.

Attention 'grabbers'

Using attention grabbers, some of which are set out below should not only improve the layout, but also allow a greater flexibility over the use of space. Just because we have a page, we do not have to fill it. Sometimes leaving an expanse of white space can be very effective . . .

can't it?

A selection of attention grabbers

- Asterisk or blob points are helpful, particularly if space is left between the points (as it is here)
- Line drawings using in-house expertise (appeal for would-be artists or cartoonists)
- Spot colour/tints
- Coloured paper

- Quotes in the middle
  of text draw the eye,
  especially in bold

- Margin notes if space is available focuses attention on key matters

- Illustrations and photographs (or collages) are worth 1,000 words. (Even words can be used as 'illustrations' in the way the case studies are displayed within this book. Breaking up pages of text in this way relieves our eyes and (hopefully!) prevents boredom.)

- **Bold quotes**

- Key words as paragraph headings (as are used throughout this book)

- | BOXES | either featuring one or a few words, or, again as in this book, larger amounts of text which attempt to create 'word-based pictures' breaking the text.

The 'permanence of print' rule applies very much to newspapers and it should not be overlooked that the document is a reflection of the organisation. Hence, its presentation and quality must accurately reflect the way in which the board wishes the world to view it, since even though newspapers are designed for internal consumption, inevitably they will find their way into the world outside. The content and copy should be clear and accurate. Mistakes of grammar and so on hardly reflect well on the sponsoring organisation.

Feedback

Although to a large extent, if employees regularly send in articles for inclusion that is a tacit indication that the document has good acceptability among the target audience, surveys of reactions can be valuable. Before checking with others, however, the editor or senior manager responsible could carry out a subjective check by answering the questions listed in the newspaper appeal review below.

Newspaper appeal review

- Overall enticement – does presentation make you want to pick it up?

- Does content reflect aims of policy document adopted?

- Is the focus and structure as was anticipated – that is, is there a proper balance of articles, business v. personal, copy v. illustrations, and does content match profile of readership determined?
- Is typeface appropriate for items being covered?
- Are headlines and sub-headlines being used to break up slabs of text?
- If no sub-headlines are used, is text broken up in other ways?
- Is overall design as was/is required?
- Is colour used appropriately? (That is not to excess.)
- Is spot colour used effectively to break up text/highlight items?
- Are tints being used as aid to colour/counter-balance black and white areas?
- Are typefaces restricted in use? (Note: Although a mixture of typefaces can be pleasing to the eye, used to excess the effect can be confusing.)
- Are columns the appropriate size to achieve a balanced page?
- Are graphics being used and are they effective?
- Are style and content appropriate to audience needs and aims of original policy?
- Are pages and whole balanced? (That is, (a) is the content of each page presented attractively and in an easy-to-read format? and (b) does the issue contain sufficient range of material that every reader is likely to find something of interest?)
- Confirm that no lines are too long (e.g. none exceed 2.5 alphabets)?
- Confirm that jargon and unnecessary verbiage are not used?
- Confirm invite to audience to contribute to next issue and means of doing so are included?
- Are named people featured representative of whole audience?
- Is there an excess of copy submitted?

Score 14 or more YES? If not, the issue needs a rethink.

Used as objectively as is possible in the circumstances, this can provide a valuable insight into how the newspaper will be received, although the editor or respondent should have a very clear idea of the target audience and their preferences. Inevitably trying to gain objective response by one or more of the variety of initiatives set out below should provide more conclusive evidence.

Obtaining objective feedback

- Editors phoned/face-to-face sample (that is a number of readers are selected at random and their views sought).

- Questionnaire is inserted in the newspaper and response sought (if anonymous replies are allowed this may provide objective views).

- The organisation's market research department is requested to survey response and attitudes.

- An outside organisation is invited to carry out a survey (again if anonymity is promised, objectivity can be generated).

- A critique is requested from an experienced external source (the disadvantage here is that preconceptions or misconceptions of the outside entity may colour the response, unless they are encouraged to gain the 'feel' of the organisation and the workforce).

139

11

Communication via appraisal

'Gaining reinforcements'

Key learning points

1 Every opportunity should be used to foster good quality communication
2 Induction, properly conducted, is a valuable foundation for later communication
3 The appraisal interview is an example of a potentially ideal communicative process
4 Objectivity in appraisal is essential.

What we have examined so far has been an array of means, processes and devices to form communication and engender feedback, basically in order to try and stimulate, as Churchill put it, 'jaw, jaw not war, war'. Basically when people are talking and trying to understand each other, then it is unlikely that simultaneously they could be at each other's throats. Of course, it is not just when we are consciously trying to communicate that we do communicate. Every act of two-way verbal or written intercourse involves us in communication. When replying, 'Don't bother me now, I'm up to my ears in this analysis', the manager in case study 1.6 was communicating with his staff. Unfortunately that was an example of negative communication as what was actually being inferred was:

- 'You are not as important as this work I am doing'
- 'I don't want to be bothered with your problems'

and, essentially,

- 'I have no wish to communicate positively with you'.

It is hardly surprising in such circumstances if the employees not only retreat, rebuffed, but also do not repeat the process. The instant 'Don't bother me now' may communicate, but also it creates an ongoing communication barrier.

The ways in which we provide both positive and negative communication are very widespread, and may commence before a person even becomes an employee. Thus, the way in which the organisation is perceived in the marketplace helps us form a picture of its philosophy and outlook. The way we are, the way we appear, the company we keep and the way we behave all say a great deal about us as individuals before we ever open our mouths – and the same is true of employers.

Case study 11.1
NOT QUITE THE REAL THING

In 1994 there was a great deal of controversy caused by one of the UK's leading food retailers, J. Sainsbury, launching its own-brand cola in a can which very closely resembled that of Coca Cola. Eventually Sainsbury changed their design but not before there had been several days of critical press coverage of the company. What was surprising was not that such a 'passing off' could be contemplated against such a major product, but that it emanated from a company with such a fine reputation. The perception of Sainsbury was that of 'market leader', 'responsible business', 'fine morals' and so on.

Key technique
People wish to be proud of the organisation for which they work and successful organisations usually have little problem obtaining recruits. People like to be associated with success. If they join on the basis that the employer has attributes that they admire, their motivation may be damaged if they find their idol has feet of clay.

141

In recruiting, the organisation moves from using its reputation formed by latent communication to actual communication. Information is provided which can either strengthen or correct external impressions. When a recruit joins, a considerable amount of information must be provided to induct the newcomer into the reality of 'the way things are done around here'. If, during this whole process, the newcomer is constantly urged to question, to clarify and to contribute, then the communication process has not only begun but been initiated in the most effective way. Pre-conceptions or misconceptions must be corrected and facts provided to supplant conjecture.

Induction

It is essential that due weight is given to the process of welcoming a new recruit to the organisation and trying to make them feel at home, since recruitment is expensive, while labour losses tend to be highest in the first year of employment. New employees have an immediate need to know and to understand the organisation they have joined – what it is, what it does and how it achieves its ends. As such, most recruits will be willing listeners and learners. Conversely, many will be somewhat reticent about speaking out and may need encouragement to do so.

142

The successful implementation of the induction process is a combination of user-friendly documentation and genuine interest from both departmental and personnel functions. It can be divided into three main areas of time as follows.

- An introduction period covering the time from the conclusion of the final interview, the period of offer and acceptance, and up to and including arrival. While care must be taken not to overload the appointee, if information can be given to them prior to the start date the process of assimilation can start that much earlier.

- An induction period covering the time from arrival to, say, the end of the second month of employment, when a great deal of information must be absorbed so that the recruit can actually begin to work and to work effectively. (Note: The end of the 2 month period link with the time limit by which a recruit must be given a statement of their terms of employment.)

- An instruction period covering the time from, say, the beginning of the third month to the end of first year of employment. The aim during this time is to enable the new employee to become completely at ease in his or her environment, increasingly productive and to lead up to their first appraisal which may generate further training needs.

Mentoring

To try to make it easy for a recruit to learn all about the organisation and to be assimilated by it, and to contribute to its life, mentors may be used. The concept of a mentor is somewhat akin to a 'mother hen' – someone who watches over the recruit, is on hand to answer their questions or concerns, yet because they are not part of the chain of command may be more approachable. The use of the system can have unexpected benefits.

Case study 11.2
BY YOUR PUPILS YOU'LL BE TAUGHT

The company had operated a mentoring system for a number of years and one of the mentors was approaching retirement. With the appointment of one of the last recruits the mentor would assist, however, a new lease of life opened up for her. Having always noted previous recruits' questions, the mentor had built up a store of information, but so interesting and detailed were the questions asked by the recruit that the mentor was forced to expand the usual reference material she had available, and was constantly asking several departments for assistance and information, and the answers virtually doubled the data she had collected. On retirement the mentor was asked by the company to write a checklist of all the questions the recruits had asked.

Key technique
By encouraging questions and feedback additional, ideally focused training material was generated.

Job descriptions

Recruits are sourced in order to carry out required functions. One of the first questions applicants need to answer concerns the exact requirements of their job. The purpose of a job description (JD) is to codify such requirements so that both employer and employee know what is required, and within which parameters or to what level of performance such tasks must be completed. Mutual agreement to the content of a job description leads to a greater understanding of what is required, a prioritisation of tasks and a recognition of skills, or a lack of such skills which may be capable of being eradicated by means of training, the provision of which can be discussed. In doing all this the two parties are forced to discuss and determine – in short to communicate. For obvious reasons the introduction of a system of job descriptions, particularly where it is required that each task is to have a measure of performance incorporated, can raise concerns among employees and needs to be handled carefully.

Introducing job descriptions

- Is there a timetable which allows adequate time for consultation and explanation of the principles and practice?

- Is there a user-friendly guide from which employees can have all their questions answered and/or management briefings at which these concerns can be identified, with explanations and reassurances provided?

- Is there to be an appeal mechanism whereby disputes can be settled by an independent third party?

- Is there to be a pilot scheme, with draft JDs agreed or discussed between subjects and superiors, while others can see the scheme in operation?

- Has sufficient time been allowed:

  (a) for explanation of the principles behind the system;

  (b) for coaching in its adoption, particularly of those who will need to compose the job descriptions;

  (c) to answer concerns and queries;

  (d) for the results of the pilot scheme to be put into operation and difficulties identified, eradicated or overcome?

- Have any benefits attaching to those with a successful assessment of attainment in accordance with the requirements of the measures of performance been arranged for the first assessment after the completion of the pilot? (Some appraisal schemes based on JD completion link additional payments to 'good' performance and reassurance may be necessary on this point.)

- Is there a mechanism for reviewing the effectiveness of the scheme, say, a year after inception?

- Is there a procedure for updating JDs and instituting new measures of performance?

Of course, setting up the type of system that will answer all these concerns is itself a communication exercise. It may be preferable for one person to oversee their production to ensure standardisation of approach. If so he or she needs to conduct a communication exercise of their own to ensure adequate input from other managers and staff. A standardised format can reduce implementation problems.

Title: Pharmacy assistant   *Grade*:

Hours: Part-time (specify number)   *Unsocial working*: YES/NO

Responsible to: Pharmacy manager   *Responsible for*: Junior

Purpose of job: Safe receipt, storage and issue of drugs and other pharmacy products to support efficient and cost-effective service, minimising wastage. Providing assistance to the pharmacy manager as required.

Specific duties:
1 Receipt checking and storage of goods in accordance with specifications and procedures.
2 Maintenance of specified stock levels, reordering when necessary from main store.
3 Preparation of departmental requisitions and recording of all issues against department code.
4 Effecting postal and alternative means deliveries to outlying customers.
5 Stock rotation in accordance with guidelines.
6 Maintenance of an 'unable to supply' record and subsequent fulfilment when stocks available.
7 Processing returns as required by procedure.
8 Keeping stores clean, tidy and well ordered.
9 Assisting in the preservation of the security of the store.
10 Updating and preserving the accuracy of the computerised stock system.
11 Working at all times to help provide a safe and effective service to the customers of the pharmacy.
12 Such other duties as may reasonably be required by the pharmacy manager.
Agreed by job holder........................ date
Agreed by manager .... date

Knowledge skills attitude and experience required:
1 Sound general education and commensurate level of intelligence.
2 Willingness to learn skills and to devote attention to detail.
3 Basic computer input skills.
4 Commitment to the principles of a caring profession.
5 Ability to work alone and in accordance with written procedures rather than with personal supervision.

145

Performance review

The use of the job description is not just to set out the list of duties and any measures of performance, though this is by far its most valuable feature. It is also to provide objective criteria against which performance can be assessed. The purposes of performance review can be stated as:

- to assess a job holder's performance and potential;
- to identify strengths and ensure these are utilised;
- to identify weaknesses and develop a coaching plan to eradicate them;
- to enable job holder and manager to achieve consensus on priorities for immediate future, establishing fresh objectives and measures as necessary. This would entail revision of the job description and the agreement of new measures of performance;
- to anticipate demands due to be made on staff as a result of likely changes in job responsibilities.

But, of course, the whole process is yet another opportunity for communication between employee and immediate superior. For that reason it needs to be allowed adequate time.

146

Case study 11.3
SQUEEZE IT IN!

The time for the annual appraisal was past and still the accounts manager had not set times for review sessions with his staff. Since he had 15 employees to assess and each interview was scheduled to last an average of 20/30 minutes he was under considerable pressure to get down to the task. After three had been completed he became irritated with the time being taken and requested all other employees to complete their own assessments which he would sign.

Key technique
While self-assessment is a valuable part of the appraisal process, it is essential that not only are the gradings allocated, discussed and agreed, but also that each employee receives guidance concerning their priorities and objectives for the next period. By dismissing this aspect, their manager was effectively dismissing them – at least in terms of being valuable enough to spend time on. It was hardly surprising that the department (also featured in case study 1.6) had such a high labour turnover.

The review of performance, particularly where the results are linked to reward (that is salary or wage increase or bonus) can be very emotive and, like introducing job descriptions, the suggestion that such a process should be implemented needs to be handled with great care and with a full communication process.

1 Introduction of process

Those primarily responsible for the scheme – the management – will need to be briefed on its aims, administration and problems, and also to be trained in conducting the process and interviews. Initially a discussion document should be distributed which will identify the main requirement and aims of the scheme. It will address:

(a) the enabling of employee and manager to systematically assess performance against preset objectives;

(b) the establishing of strengths and weaknesses, and from that a training need;

(c) the means by which aims and targets for the following period are set and measured;

(d) the establishing of career paths;

(e) he objective and supportive role required of the assessors;

(f) the need for full communication and consultation with employees to enable the positive aspects of the scheme to be attained;

(g) how the administration of the scheme will operate, including the appeals procedure;

(h) (depending on existing training arrangements) how the training needs identified from the scheme will be addressed.

2 Proposals re format, procedure, appeal

From this forum the outline scheme will be defined, certain problems and their solutions identified, and the administration clarified. These points need to be codified into a guidance 'crib' for management. The scheme then needs to be communicated to and discussed with the workforce. This should fall into two parts:

■ an initial written document setting out objectives and administration etc. of the scheme, which will give employees time to consider their concerns and questions; and

■ meetings at which employees will be able to discuss the scheme.

It is essential that this process is as open as possible, since without the commitment of the employees to the process, it cannot work. It may be necessary to make reassurances or guarantees regarding the maintenance

147

of wage increases, and opportunities for those with a poor review to have 'another chance' etc. If the scheme is to be tied to a bonus or wage review, that dimension must also be addressed.

3 Concept training

As a result of this process the scheme format may have been somewhat changed and it may be necessary to rebrief the management. Coaching may need to be repeated, since it is essential that all those involved in carrying out interviews should attend, with the aim that within the organisation all interviews should be conducted on a similar basis.

4 Pilot scheme

This will have the effect of highlighting difficulties in the scheme within the organisation, and will allow both employees and managers a chance to try the system, before full implementation. The results of the pilot – including difficulties and their resolution – should be publicised and explained.

The benefits of the scheme are long term and considerable, and can only be attained if the scheme works properly, thus time spent in planning and perfecting the scheme should be a sound investment.

To generate the discussion that is an essential part of the process, a form, the detail of which should be discussed as part of the introductory process, should be utilised. It may be that the process is restricted to supervisory staff or above, in which case the following example may be appropriate. For more junior employees a shorter and simpler form may be preferable in order to ensure the complexity of the form itself does not deter participants from participating fully.

PERFORMANCE REVIEW FORM

Managerial/supervisory staff   Performance review (PR)

(Note: Some questions may require a commentary style answer. If space is insufficient please use a continuation sheet.)

PART 1 Background

Name   Position
Department   Date appointed to position
PR form issue date   Interview held

Is the job description for this position up to date and correct? If not, please specify the area(s) in which it is deficient.

If there are changes, are you able to cope with the altered responsibilities – or do you require training in order to cope?

If so, please specify what type of training

Have you, since the date of your last review, undertaken any training? If so, please give details, assess the worth of the training and state how it is helping you in your job.

Is it likely that there will be changes to your responsibilities before the next review? If so, do you feel you will be able to cope with these changes or will you require training? If so, please indicate the areas where training may be necessary.

Are there any personal factors which could have an effect on your performance in the near future? If so, please provide details.

Is there any other information which you feel has a bearing on this review process and/or the performance of the job? If so, please provide details.

In the chart set out below, list the measures of performance for each of the duties set out in your job description and then on a grading scale of A to E (A meaning you have always achieved the standard set in the measure; B means these standards have usually been achieved; C sometimes achieved; D seldom achieved; E never achieved).

		Rating
Position objectives	Measures of performance	A B C D E
1.		
2.		
3.	(Data derived from job description)	
4.		
5.		

If you have graded yourself D or E for any of the duties, please state for each why you feel you have performed at this level.

General

Did you achieve anything else within the period which is not covered by your job description? If so, please give details.

Was there anything you needed which would have improved your performance? If so, please give details.

Have you been able to help any colleague with his work? If so, please give details.

Are you able to deal with all requirements for information concerned with your job from:

- superior   YES/NO   ■ colleagues   YES/NO
- other internal   YES/NO   ■ external sources   YES/NO

If the answer to any of these is NO, please state why you feel this was the case.

Do you feel you are able to get on with those with whom you come into contact?

What do you feel is (are) your main strength(s)?

What do you feel is (are) your main weakness(es)?

On the scale on the previous page (i.e. A to E), how do you rate yourself for the following?

Accuracy:	Diligence:
Setting priorities:	Relationships:
Motivation:	Adaptability:
Commitment:	Overall performance:

Part 2

A performance review interview with .... was held on ....
at .... The assessment provided by the job holder was reviewed and the ratings confirmed/altered as shown.
The overall performance rating was agreed as .... (A to E). Please set out an analysis of any action(s) agreed to be implemented, giving measures of performance and timescales if appropriate.

1.
2. etc.

Training needs: please set out the type of training required and, if relevant, the timing of such training.

Signed ....Job holder

....Manager

....Date

Reviewed by ....Director ....Date

The completion of the performance review form and procedure, which depends essentially on a dialogue between employee and manager, tends to generate requirements for training. Again a discussion of these requirements and how they are best satisfied aids the communication process. The underlying message being conveyed is that the employer is committed to the employee and the development of the employee's talents. This should help generate the employee's interest in and commitment to the organisation and its future. Since both the employee and their dependants have a vested interest in the survival of the organisation, that vested interest can be exploited to gain commitment.

Informal review

The foregoing describes the process of a formal review process, which with a large number of employees may be necessary, if only to try to ensure that the whole workforce is treated similarly and indeed that there is a process to force regular communication. The wise manager (and great communicator) will not, however, wait until a review session to guide his or her staff. The best means of review and appraisal is the informal on-the-spot coaching of the employee to perform the job to the best of their ability. In the same way that the 'best manure is the farmer's boot', the best appraisal is the friendly word. Praise can be a powerful motivator and should be administered at any time. If the process of 'walking the job' or 'management by walking about' is used, this technique lends itself to informal guidance.

151

Case study 11.4
DO AS I DO

The director had come in on the end of an argument between the shift manager and one of his team. 'What's the trouble with her?' the director asked. 'No idea' replied the manager 'but she has been late twice this week, is constantly asking to go to the cloakroom, and doesn't seem to be paying attention – so I've told her unless she bucks her ideas up, she's for the high jump.'

The director made no comment, but spent some time with the manager who had a poor 'personnel-management' reputation and whose team performance was under target. During their discussion, the director explored all the problems being experienced by the manager and made some suggestions regarding possible solutions. At the end of their discussion he enquired whether the manager had found the talk helpful. The manager was enthusiastic, particularly as he had had an opportunity to discuss problems and had gained some suggested solutions to try out. 'Yes', replied the director 'when we invest time considering these matters, there is often a payback. Now I suggest that you call that person back in here and ask her if she has any problems bothering her. You've little to lose and you might find that giving her the opportunity to discuss things may gain her support which merely criticising will not.'

Key technique

In fact the woman's husband was seriously ill in hospital and she wanted to check his progress regularly by phone. The manager knew nothing of this, was mortified to discover it and immediately arranged matters so that she could telephone regularly. He also arranged counselling.

Applying the stick can generate output, but little commitment. It can also create problems where, to 'repay' such unfairness, employees can deliberately interpret instructions without using common sense. Trying to generate commitment by investing time in people helps win their will as well as their bodies and to win we need to win wills. 'He that complies against his will, is of his own opinion still' (from 'Hudibrass' by Samuel Butler) – no conversion of minds or gathering of commitment will have been achieved here.

In the UK the tendency is to criticise too readily and give praise too infrequently. This is odd since being praised is an understandable and widespread human desire, and we all know how much better a little praise or recognition can make us feel, how much our self-confidence can be bolstered and how much more motivated we feel. While criticism has been levelled at the length of the credits at the end of films and television programmes, one major advantage must surely be the motivational effect of recognising all those who played a part in the production, no matter how small. Perhaps it might help employee commitment and employee communication if there were far more personal recognition in corporate documentation. Restricting such recognition purely to the board may be very short-sighted – knowing one's efforts will be recognised could be a powerful motivation to perform well.

In the *Water Babies*, Charles Kingsley wrote of the 'loveliest fairy in the world and her name is Mrs Doasyouwouldbedoneby'. If we like receiving praise, we should be ready to provide it. Indeed, if we give praise when it is due (and even sometimes when strictly it is not), not only are we engendering a communication process, since we may well obtain feedback from the subject, but also we are making it that much more easy for ourselves should we eventually have to criticise. If we only ever criticise, the effectiveness of our words will eventually be lost. If, however, we give praise when it is due and brickbats when they are due, a sense of proportion and fairness is generated and, even though people may not like being criticised, they may be more prepared to accept criticism and to heed it because they know it emanates from a source which sees and acknowledges both sides of the effectiveness of their activities. 'Praise me, scold me – just never ignore me.'

12

Countering the opposition

'Friendly fire'

Key learning points

1 Some employees are prepared to work against their employer's interests
2 Procedures can minimise the effects of such negative commitment
3 Granting employees a stake in the ownership of the employer may help improve attitudes, and reduce waste and loss
4 Solutions rather than castigation need to be sought for problem employees.

Friendly fire is the polite euphemism given to the adverse action of one's own side. The damage occasioned by such attacks causing loss to one's own forces, not only partially destroys our own effectiveness as an effective fighting force, but also saps morale. During the D-Day invasion and subsequent battle for the control of Normandy, the US air force gained a reputation for being somewhat careless with its fire-power and causing a considerable number of casualties in its own forces, an event which has sadly been repeated in a number of other conflicts. Suffering losses from the enemy is of great concern, but can have the effect of binding together the defendants (as it did in the London Blitz).

It is vital to recognise that even though we may have all the procedures and commitment to positive employee communications and involvement, there may be an element in the workforce who have other priorities and take adverse action.

'The easiest way to make more money is to stop losing it'

In every economic activity, on each occasion that resources are committed, decisions are made, often so instinctively that there is no awareness that alternatives have been considered, if, indeed, they have. The choice is between the retention of resources, usually cash or capital, and expenditure. In the one-person business, the owner has total control over expenditure and, thus, the progress or otherwise of the business. Loss or waste in this situation is entirely under the owner's control and will often depend on the quality of decisions taken. To a large extent, the careful commitment of scarce resources as a result of such decisions can be the difference between a small business remaining small and a small business becoming medium sized.

Making poor or bad decisions is likely to be costly, and could be the difference between growth and stagnation. Yet many decisions taken in business are based on inadequate information and communication, following insufficient consideration of the problem, and with an imprecise understanding of the implications or effects of the decision.

155

Loss of entrepreneurial choice

Few sole traders are content to remain as such, and most wish to expand and increase their return. To do so, business size must be increased and, as it does, the owner's absolute control over expenditure, as well as the management of, and decisions concerning, resources, becomes diluted. This control, which we can call 'entrepreneurial choice', must, as the business grows, be delegated to employees, whose knowledge and understanding of the priorities of the business will usually be less perfect than that of the owner – and, sad to say, some of whom will have a 'hidden agenda' which may be opposed to the aims of the business. Almost inevitably, the degree of 'discomfort' of work, which the owner was prepared to accept in the expectation of increased returns, becomes sublimated for a more 'comfortable' style of work, generating lower profits, by those who are working for a wage. Further, some employees will realise that a proportion of the assets may be able to be converted to their own purposes.

Once entrepreneurial choice and control is removed from a profit-earner to a wage-earner, the level of profit earned may diminish, waste tends to increase and so does loss from theft, whether this be of time, materials or cash. Controls are essential in this regard and the kind of authority chart, of which an extract is set out below, should be implemented and strictly adhered to.

AUTHORITY LEVELS CHART (EXTRACT ONLY)

It is essential for the proper control of the organisation that approval is granted to contracts by suitably appointed personnel, and for the allocation and disposal of money and stock assets of the organisation that authority is granted at an appropriate level.

CONTRACTS
All contracts between the company and third parties, other than those covered by items set out below, must be channelled through the company secretary's office, to ensure correct status (that is whether it is to be regarded as a Deed or not) and approval. The company secretary will arrange the passing of suitable board resolutions granting approval to specified person(s) to sign on behalf of the company. It should be noted that sufficient time to obtain such a resolution should be allowed.

CASH COMMITMENT
Capital projects:
Authority for all projects (note: no low cutoff)   Board
(Items must be supported by a capital expenditure
(Capex) form)

Repairs and renewals, purchase of furniture and fittings
(All items must be supported by a Capex form)
Up to £1,000   Manager – level ..
Over £1,000 and up to £5,000   Director
Over £5,000   Board

Vehicles
(Supported by Capex form, for new allocations, or
replacement form for write-offs and replacements)   Board
All purchases to be in accordance with policy

Expense items
Up to £500   Manager – level ..
Over £500 and up to £1,000   Senior manager
Over £1,000 and up to £5,000   Director
Over £5,000   Board

Committed expenditure
Rent, rates, utility costs – where no change
or increase is less than rate of inflation   Manager – level ..
Where change has taken place   Director

Bought ledger
Raw materials, services, etc., in accordance
with budgeted level of production   Purchase manager
Not in accordance with level of production   Director

Wage adjustments
Annual review   Board
Other than annual review, or for new staff,
or replacement at other than at old rate
Salary up to £10,000 p.a.   Manager – level ..
Salary over £10,000 p.a.   Board
and so on for each item of expenditure

The absence of such controlling authority not only leads to confusion as to 'who can sign for what', but also indicates to those who are interested in exploiting the business for their own interests, that such exploitation is likely to be relatively easy to achieve.

Case study 12.1
CHECKING IT OUT

The director was speaking to a consultant and boasting that he kept his finger very much on the pulse of the business, and his controls were 'pretty near waterproof'. 'Do you know', he said, 'I sign every cheque, so I know exactly what is going on?'

The consultant commented that this was an effective control but it was not sufficient. 'Why not?' demanded the director. 'Although the fact that the staff know that you sign the cheques should help control some cash-fraud and so forth, it does not stop over-ordering by mistake or by design (where the person placing the order is in partnership with the supplier to pocket part of the gain). What you should be doing is controlling the placing of orders. To a large extent signing the cheque is a routine mechanical act, the contract is binding when the order is placed. You signed a cheque last month, for the supply of stationery . . .'

'That was fine, I made a point of checking the delivery myself.' 'Oh the delivery was in accordance with the order, but did you really want to have about eight years' supply of stationery, at a time when your cashflow is tight?'

Key technique
All aspects of controls need investigating and the point that there are controls brought to the attention of all involved.

157

The opportunity to convert the assets of the business to personal use may be offset to some extent by making employees joint owners in the business (a fact recently recommended for consideration by more employers by the EU). The aim is to encourage greater accountability, and engendering improved care of choice and decision making, and even greater care of the assets.

Case study 12.2
'NOW IT'S MINE, I'LL TAKE GREATER CARE'

Maynards PLC was one of the first companies to introduce an employee share ownership scheme. The company had already carried out a great deal of work on employee communication and involvement, including explaining the economic facts of life to all employees. Productivity had increased and wastage had been reduced. Making the employees shareholders, however, added a dimension to the relationship, which many greeted positively, showing dedication to 'improving things generally'.

The reaction of one woman in one of the factories was typical. She was noticed tidying a pile of packaging, some of which had fallen into a gangway. Previously the attitude would either have been to ignore the mess or to wait until it had been damaged by passing traffic and then to throw it away as rubbish. She, however, spent several minutes of her tea break, smoothing the fallen items and reinserting them into the pile so that the weight would remove the creases. When a manager thanked her for her efforts her reply was 'Now I own part of this place, I'm going to look after it'.

Key technique
Not all employees will have the same positive attitude and neither will a change of attitudes from apathetic or negative to positive be achieved swiftly. It takes time and continual investment to change attitudes.

Postscript
Wastage at the same factory had been running at a high level and it was suspected that pilfering was taking place. Some time after the share ownership scheme was introduced, two or three anonymous tips were received by the management concerning activities of some employees. As a result there were several dismissals for theft.

However, joint ownership is very rarely an accurate description of the relationship of the employee to the organisation, and even in organisations such as the John Lewis Partnership, where the equity, and thus the profit, is employee-owned, or NFC, where the employees still own around 50 per cent of the equity, employees are also paid a salary or wage. Human nature being what it is, even though some employees may be totally committed to the concept of optimum expenditure to reap optimum profit for the good of the business (if only to protect long-term employment), not all will be so committed or careful, and waste, over-expenditure and reduced accountability, is almost inevitable.

Communication can play a valuable part in trying to offset the almost inevitable loss of high returns, but it cannot provide the whole answer.

The vicious circle

Unfortunately theft from businesses, be it of time, raw materials, assets or services is on the increase. Some estimate the loss to businesses from staff theft and fraud to be as high as 5 per cent of sales, and such losses are, of course, a straight deduction from profit. Indeed, since many businesses only make profits of around 5 per cent of sales, it could be argued either that the losses equal the profits or that, were such losses not incurred, profits could be doubled.

In Chapter 4, we looked at the PIE circle, which recommended encouraging the development of commitment through communication to generate pride from inspiration and enthusiasm. That was the positive benefit circle. We can use another circle to demonstrate a problem currently affecting most employers – the vicious circle of staff theft.

159

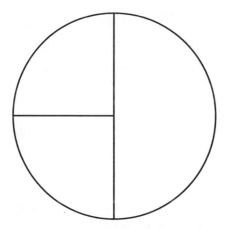

Figure 12.1 The staff honesty/dishonesty circle

In Figure 12.1 there are three portions. One-quarter of the circle illustrates the 25 per cent of staff who are completely honest, the other quarter, the 25 per cent of staff who are dishonest, while the half circle represents the 50 per cent of staff who are as honest or dishonest as the company's procedures and controls will let them be. In this it is essential that controls are widely discussed, the reasons they are required are explained and general commitment to the concept is obtained. If employees are involved in the introduction of the controls, the goodwill of the majority should outweigh any backlash from the minority.

Case study 12.3
SEARCH ME

Theft problems had multiplied at the organisation which produced a high value and very portable product. A 'planted' employee's first report indicated that as many as 30 per cent of the employees might be involved in stealing.

The management decided to give the matter a high profile and, taking the line that thefts and wastage of product could seriously damage the prospects for the long-term employment of the whole workforce, involved the trade union representatives in the discussions. The company indicated that the following year's wage increase could be imperilled by the continuing losses and eventually, apparently from the union representatives, came the suggestion that a policy of random searches should be implemented. Working with the union representatives, a complete procedure and implementation timetable was formulated, and then implemented with hardly any problems.

Key technique
The company wanted to introduce the search policy but knew if it had tried to do this without union support, the backlash could ruin the idea. Gently manipulating the representatives so that they thought it was their idea, granted the idea added credence and the plan enhanced acceptability. Wastage from theft dropped swiftly and the following year's wage increase was protected.

Introducing such controls should be publicised as much for the need to protect the innocent as to catch the guilty. In the company in case study 12.3, the fact that 'my rise depends on your thieving' (since almost inevitably some employees are aware of the acts of others, but through a misguided sense of loyalty will not report them) was widely used to gain acceptance of the search routine. Further, the previous understanding that if caught a thief would 'get away with' the first offence was dropped and the rule that 'theft would lead to dismissal and prosecution' was adopted.

Case study 12.4
ME TOO

The company in case study 3.3 investigated the fraud perpetrated by two members of the wages department and found that they had obtained in excess of £25,000 over the period of a year. So concerned was the company at the potential adverse publicity, that it decided not to prosecute the individuals, to the outrage of many of the other employees. One of the most outspoken critics was in charge of the bought ledger department and, about a year later, a further investigation discovered that he had been passing invoices for goods not received or not received to the value stated and splitting the gain with suppliers with whom he was in collusion.

Key technique
Allowing it to be understood that employees have a 'free go' is tantamount to inviting theft. The response of the bought ledger supervisor was 'Well, all I have to lose is my job – and I only lose that if you find me out'. This attitude can swiftly spread through the entire organisation. While some will not be encouraged to steal, nevertheless their morale, commitment and motivation can be severely sapped. This is adverse communication – and sadly the messages seem to be far more swiftly understood.

161

Poor performers

Employees who steal from the organisation are actively destroying what could be their own livelihood and cannot be said to be in any way committed to the organisation. Some employees, however, may be wholly committed to the organisation and yet unable to perform to the standard required of them by their supervision. Such employees are not working against the aims of the organisation, but are simply unable to work with it in the way that is required. The standard means of communication to try and motivate them is unlikely to work since there is a barrier through which messages, invitations and exhortations cannot pass. The key to dealing with such a reaction from problem employees is to try to ascertain the cause using a problem performers checklist such as the one set out below.

Examine the problem

- **The employee**
    - (a) Is person new to job?
    - (b) Is person new to type of work?
    - (c) Is person new to country/part of country?
    - (d) Has person adequate reading/speaking skills?
        - (i) in native language?
        - (ii) in language used at workplace?
    - (e) Is person under stress or suffering from personal problems?
    - (f) Is person under medical supervision?
    - (g) Are there any housing/travel difficulties?
    - (h) Is there any evidence of disaffection regarding the department, employer etc. (for example the employee could be smarting from being passed over for promotion, or at not gaining a pay rise, or recognition for a valuable suggestion implemented, and so on)?

- **Training**
    - (a) Has person been present at training courses?
    - (b) Has there been any apparent problem in acceptability on course?
    - (c) Is training undertaken willingly or with resentment?
    - (d) Have courses been assessed for validity and effectiveness?

- **Relationships**
    - (a) Is person a loner?
    - (b) Do they have problems interrelating to other employees?
    - (c) Is there any evidence of harassment, discrimination, victimisation?
    - (d) Has management/supervision changed recently?
    - (e) Does employee seem to have workplace friends?

- **Position**
    - (a) Is position appropriate to person's skills, experience, capability?
    - (b) Is task boring or repetitive (if so, is it possible to rotate employees so that all share in this task and others which are more interesting)?
    - (c) Are working conditions poor?
    - (d) Are working hours unsocial or difficult?
    - (e) Are rewards reasonable compared to other jobs in workplace, in neighbouring employers?

(Note: This list is not meant to be exhaustive.)

In trying to assess the nature of the problem by requiring answers to the questions, an impression will be built both of the employee and of the way they are fitting (or failing to fit) into the fabric of the business. Such facts should highlight the main areas of difficulty and suggest that concentrated attention should be paid to these. Unless such facts are available effective remedial action will be virtually impossible to implement.

Stress

It has been estimated that at any one time as many as 20 per cent of the workforce of the average organisation will be coping with, or trying to cope with, a personal problem that is likely to affect their performance. Of these nearly half (which is thus just under 10 per cent of the total workforce) will be experiencing a serious problem, such as divorce, death or serious illness of a close relative, or friend, court case and so on. All such problems cause stress which is not only detrimental to the output of the employee, but also is likely to affect the output of their colleagues. This can be compounded by unsympathetic attitudes of those in any position of authority who, in trying to achieve output or targets, may feel their efforts are being negated, virtually deliberately, by those suffering from stress. Unlike a broken leg, or a heavy cold, stress symptoms are far less obvious and thus more difficult to discern and counter.

163

Stress-related illnesses accounted for over a third of certified absence in the UK in 1991. The contributory reasons, while important in their own context, are irrelevant here; what should concern us is the effect on morale and commitment, both of the sufferer and their colleagues, and the consequent effect that it has on the business.

Case study 12.5
FUELLING HER PROBLEMS

The driver at the petrol station was very annoyed since he felt the cashier had been most offhand to him. At the end of the protracted transaction he remarked to the cashier that she should be careful as her attitude could offend customers who might then shop elsewhere. He was so concerned that he complained to the company operating the service station and was told that earlier in her shift the cashier had been told that the company were making her redundant.

Key technique
It is hardly surprising if problems are generated or aggravated if staff are left to cope (particularly in this instance where the employee was operating on her own) in such circumstances. Suitable cover should have been provided or notification of the information delayed until the end of the cashier's shift. The insensitivity of some managements is staggering – *'doasyouwouldbedoneby' is far from their consideration.*

In a 1993 report for the Health and Safety at Work Executive, Professor Tom Cox of Nottingham University recommended that stress at work, which it is estimated costs 90 million lost working days in the UK each year, should be regarded as a health and safety issue.

In addition to the costs of lost productive days, the potential extra damage to an employer's business if employees suffering from stress are required to cope, rather than being helped and solutions sought, is considerable. No doubt many of Henry V's men were suffering from stress, particularly having marched 250 miles in 17 days and having already fought one battle to win Harfleur. High profile communication and sound man-management helped overcome many of the problems that were no doubt bubbling under the surface then – and so it is today.

Counselling

The busy manager can perhaps be excused for being irritated that some of his or her staff are unable to perform at the level required, even where this is due to genuine and real problems. Being realistic, however, it is essential to build in to any required output figures the fact that, reflecting the above research, some members of the team will not from time to time be able to perform to peak output. This can actually be due to a variety of causes.

Case study 12.6
AVOIDING THE LAST STRAW

In the summer of 1994 the quality of air in and around London was much poorer than acceptable levels. A combination of low winds, high temperatures and humidity at a time of year when there was traditionally a high pollen count created a situation where many people, not normally affected by breathing difficulties, found it difficult to perform adequately. A number of rail strikes added to the misery of travellers as well as worsening the poor air quality from the increased use of commuters' cars. The team in the export company, faced with all these problems and a large order to arrange in a short time, virtually mutinied – a reaction caused as much by frustration as by a reaction to the difficulties.

Their manager took them all out to a local pub with an air-conditioned room to discuss the situation. Rather than throwing the question at them initially, he let them unwind for 30 minutes or so, chatting about the World Cup, Wimbledon and other activities then in the news, and provided refreshments. Having, by a combination of cool temperatures, a removal from the stress of the workplace and a little alcohol, gained calmness, he moved the discussion on to their present problems and invited any ideas. 'The only time I feel like working at the moment is at night' joked one of the employees. 'Why not?' replied the manager. 'It's cooler, your travel problems will be minimised and you can rest at home during the day – how does everyone feel about it?' The more the discussion continued the more enthusiasm there was for the idea which was eventually adopted. The deadline for the large export order was met easily and most of the aggravation endured in working through the day was avoided.

High profile = high risk

High profile management can help raise morale and commitment, particularly since it tends to be associated with successful entities (the less successful tend to keep their heads down). However, being high profile incurs a real possibility of damage should an unwise word be uttered.

165

Case study 12.7
SHOT IN THE FOOT

In 1990, as part of a presentation to the Institute of Directors, Gerald Ratner, then chairman of Ratners, an international publicly quoted company he had built from virtually nothing, referred humorously to some of the products his chain sold as 'crap' and others as 'only as valuable as a sandwich from Marks & Spencer'.

The remark was intended humorously but the immediate damage it caused to the company was enormous. The share price plunged from 192p to 8p, Ratner had to give up the chairmanship and then his directorship, and eventually, having closed around 200 units, the company name was changed to Signet.

The damage was caused by the perception planted in the minds of the customers that what they were spending their money on was rubbish or next to worthless. Similarly the effect on the employees was marked. To the customers they were associated with rubbish products, to their friends they became a butt of humour, while, apparently, to the chairman, their interests counted for little. This is hardly the way to generate motivation, particularly of those at the sharp end, remote from direct 'hands-on' supervision of senior management and who you require to sell products that the chairman regards as 'crap'.

How to be a great communicator

He who communicates may lead, but he who communicates without careful assessment of the effect of the words on all involved, can destroy any claim he may have to lead – and may accurately direct some horrifyingly effective 'friendly fire' on his own forces.

13

Problem solving

'Dealing with defaulters'

Key learning points

1 Human failings are inevitable and must be allowed for, and, where appropriate, assistance provided
2 Introducing new restrictions, such as 'no smoking' rules, needs careful planning and discussion to ensure positive reactions
3 Providing a counselling service can be of assistance and can also aid effective communication
4 A counselling service can improve efficiency and relationships, but needs to be marketed to achieve effectiveness.

We often overlook the fact that until relatively recently, other than a few religious days, the concept of taking a holiday in the western world was unknown – and in many parts of the world this is still the case. It can be argued that societies become more affluent by virtue of their citizens generating earnings that are surplus to immediate life-supporting requirements, which then become available for 'luxuries' such as holidays. The quid pro quo for such affluence, however, seems to be an increased pace and pressure of life itself, so much so that in many cases the same citizens feel pressurised to take a holiday, simply to be able to 'recharge their batteries' or some other phrase indicating the need for a change from the status quo before they feel able to resume normal activities. Obviously some are more affected than others, nevertheless it does seem, as we saw in Chapter 12, that stress plays an ever-increasing role in our lifestyle. Unfortunately not all those subject to stress are able to cope with it, either by virtue of their own metabolism not being affected or by taking a break so that they return refreshed. Further, the character of some people can encourage the incidence of stress and the would-be great communicator needs to respond in different ways to different people and their attitudes.

Case study 13.1
WHOSE RESPONSIBILITY?

The chairman needed an immediate response to an enquiry for a large order from overseas. He asked A – a very aggressive manager – who replied that as he was completely snowed under there was no way in which he could do the job. He asked B – whose attitude was not so much aggressive as assertive. She replied that the only way she could do the job was to defer something else as she had a number of equally urgent priorities. So the chairman asked C who he knew would do the job – because he always did. C replied that he had intended taking a day's holiday, but would postpone this and do the work. Some time later C collapsed and was away from work for some weeks.

Key technique
Being a submissive individual, C always accepted whatever was asked of him and his very character put him under what was eventually an unacceptable pressure. His chairman should have realised this and, had there been more effective communication between the two, no doubt would have done. Placing the pressure of demand first is understandable and will work in the short term, but possibly at the expense of long-term capability.

Countering the problem

Those suffering stress sometimes use a number of means of countering the effects. Unfortunately these often create their own problems and have serious side-effects which can result in a situation worse than the original.

Case study 13.2
ATTENTION HICCUP

The director was bemused since although one of her staff could be extremely conscientious, provide accurate work and appear very willing, often work was presented in a careless fashion and she seemed unwilling to contribute effectively to the work of the department. She began to make notes of the occasions on which poor work and attitude was evident, and then began looking for evidence of other facts occurring at the same time. It soon became clear that the occasions when careless work was carried out tended to be in the afternoons and followed the employee going to the local pub for lunch. The director then interviewed the 'problem employee's' colleagues and discovered that she had an alcohol problem in that as soon as she had more than one drink she tended to become hazy. 'But why does she have more than one drink on these occasions?' 'Because her husband has a job which takes him away for a week at a time every six to eight weeks, and she can't stand the solitude when he is away' came the reply.

Key technique
Having heard that the sloppy work was caused by inebriation, many managers might have left their superficial investigation there. However, in probing further the director found the real, rather than the apparent, reason. The apparent reason could have been dealt with by suggesting the employee did not go to the pub for lunch. This at least would have avoided some of the 'liquor effect' which was the prime cause of the careless work. But it would merely have added to the anxiety of the employee, who presumably found some tension relief in her alcohol intake. By using communication techniques to uncover the 'reason behind the reason', action far more appropriate and effective than banning lunchtime imbibing could be taken. In this case the company had a 'personal problem' programme which provided an opportunity for employees to discuss problems in confidence with retained experts in various fields.

169

So serious has the use of alcohol become that many employers now ban its use in working hours. It is not simply a case of causing poor work, its use is inherently dangerous in many instances, particularly where the process uses machinery or requires the employee to drive and so on. There is a further dimension to this problem where the person consuming alcohol is in a position of authority. Unfortunately, because the substance is addictive, the subject may, despite the most earnest wish to break themselves of the habit, find this very difficult.

Case study 13.3
MORE ALCOHOL PROBLEMS

The accountant was accustomed to having a liquid lunch at the local pub. The director was concerned at the possible repercussions.

'Michael, I wanted to have a word with you about your lunchtime arrangements. I understand that you always have lunch at the local pub – is that right?'

'Sure – I have a few beers and a sandwich down there.'

'How do you get there and how many beers is a few?'

'I pop down in my car. I suppose I have three or four pints usually. I'm never late back.'

'Yes, I appreciate that you only take the allowed time – I'm not worried about that. What concerns me is that you are driving a company vehicle after a drinking session, and that you then start the afternoon having had a fair number of drinks.'

'It doesn't impair my work ability.'

'I agree that I haven't noticed any problems with your work. But what concerns me is the attitude of your staff.'

'Why – who's complained?'

'No one has complained – that's the trouble. Most of them seem to think it's a bit of a joke, although others don't think driving a car after having downed a few pints is any laughing matter, and I must say I agree with them.'

'Oh, I see.'

'I'm not sure if you do – because if you did I think you would avoid the problem. You are a manager and as such have a position which should command respect from your staff. If your actions are such that you are not engendering such respect, then your position as a manager is threatened. Indeed, it goes further than that since the respect for management generally also suffers, since we are seen to be condoning such actions, by not doing anything about it.'

'Oh.'

'In addition, should you need to discipline a member of your staff after lunch you will do so with your breath smelling of beer, which could undermine the authority of that disciplinary meeting, while the fact that you have been drinking itself could raise problems. Your authority itself could be undermined. Can I suggest you think about it for a couple of days and we have another chat next Monday?'

Key technique

The director has not administered any disciplinary action – merely put certain facts and derived thoughts before the accountant. Full communication of all aspects of the problem has been achieved and the discovery of a solution has been left with the accountant to determine. Obviously the director will expect some reaction at the next meeting, but if this emanates from the accountant it is likely to be more effective than any stricture from the director. Self-analysis and judgement is usually more effective than imposed requirements.

The dangers of alcohol addiction apply to employees, to fellow employees and to the assets of the employer. Explaining this from the safety and authority considerations may enable progress to a 'no alcohol' rule to be made relatively easily. However, it is vital, if such a rule is imposed, that it applies to all. There is nothing more likely to cause aggravation and even flouting of such a rule than the knowledge that, despite it, alcohol is available in the directors' dining room. It is strange, considering how difficult it can be to promulgate other messages, how quickly communication of this fact spreads throughout an organisation! Most organisations adopting a ban have become completely dry, although as part of an employee empowerment process (see Chapter 15) IBM has recently relaxed its total alcohol ban, leaving it to employees to determine the appropriateness. Experience indicates that, left to determine their own rules, employees can impose stricter requirements than many managements would suggest.

Realistic application

171

The fact that there is a no-alcohol rule should obviously apply in all cases during working hours. However, where working hours are completed and consumption takes place on the premises, there needs to be a realistic application of the rules. This is even more necessary when there is a social club (with a licensed bar) on the premises. In such circumstances rules, ensuring that having 'clocked off' or in some other way confirmed that the working day or shift has been completed, need to be implemented so that there is a clear break in everyone's mind between the hours of work and relaxation. Such differentiation is necessary to ensure that cases such as *Weetabix Ltd* v. *Criggie and Williamson* do not proliferate. In that case the Employment Appeals Tribunal found the dismissal of two employees for drinking unfair and too severe a penalty in the circumstances. The employees had arranged to go fishing straight after the conclusion of the day's work and had taken all their equipment, including beer and food for the trip to work intending to go fishing straight from work. The trip was called off, and after the end of their shift and before they went home, they sat in the rest room and consumed the beer.

In such an instance, indeed in all cases when there is a problem, full investigation of the circumstances should made before a decision is made – one example of many situations where sound communication is also sound industrial relations.

Problem meeting checklist

- Find the facts before the meeting, including as many personal details as possible. Knowing some personal details will aid rapport, and encourage a feeling that here is someone who understands and cares.

- Although a one-to-one meeting is helpful, this may be impractical if the two parties are of different sexes and the subject matter is personal, but the intervention of a third party should not be forced on the subject who may resent such an intervention

- Be tactful and allow plenty of time – including the possibility of a short recess.

- Provide refreshments, and allow those who wish to smoke, to do so. To those who smoke the opportunity to do so when discussing problems may be a valuable method of relaxing them in order to encourage a discussion of the problem. If there is a site 'No smoking rule', either a discussion room provided for such a purpose should be exempt from the requirements or the discussion should take place 'off-site'.

- Ensure the interview is confidential and protected from unwarranted intrusion.

- Try to move to some solution, however skeletal.

- In case of ongoing personal problems try to arrange for referral to experts (for example, Samaritans, doctors, solicitors and so on).

- Take notes of what transpires.

- Keep immediate superior informed of progress.

- Update on progress as necessary.

172

In conducting such an interview, the overriding rule should be that the employer takes a reactive not proactive role in order to grant and preserve the self-respect of the employee.

Smoking

Many employers are now seeking to bring smoking bans into operation at the workplace, either affecting the whole operation or premises, or at least major parts of it. As long ago as 1981 the Trades Union Congress called on affiliated unions to 'undertake a programme of education and information on smoking and health for the benefit of their members and advised unions to negotiate non-smoking areas in work-places, time off to attend smoking withdrawal courses and workplace disincentive programmes' (from the booklet 'Smoking policies at work', Institute of Personnel and Development, formerly the Institute of Personnel Management).

More recently a 1993 ruling by the European Court of Justice found that the health of an employee was perceived to have been damaged by latent smoking – that is exposure as a non-smoker to smoke from her colleagues' cigarettes. The effect of the employee breathing in smoke was classified as an industrial accident leaving her entitled to recompense. Partly as a result, the Health and Safety Executive has issued a booklet 'Passive smoking at work' which, among other matters, recommends that employers should give priority to non-smokers who do not wish to breathe tobacco smoke.

While, to a non-smoker, the imposition of a smoking ban may be seen as a relatively minor step, to a smoker addicted to nicotine, the thought of being forced to do without regular intakes of the drug can be extremely fraught. Introducing a smoking ban thus needs to be carried out over a timespan and with consideration for all involved.

173

Where the organisation is engaged on food production, or handling food, or food substitute raw materials, perfumes and flavours, or uses highly flammable products, a ban on smoking rarely causes problems, as the logic of the danger of fire and/or smoke damaging the product is inescapable. With other organisations the logic of it being better for the health of all, safer for the protection of goods and workforce, and cleaner in terms of the workplace itself, needs to be used as a basis to educate the workforce in general and smokers in particular. Despite it being obvious to a large majority of the target audience, this does not mean that the normal rules regarding effective communication should be ignored.

Follow this checklist for implementing a no smoking policy.

INTRODUCTION OF SMOKING BAN

1 Communicate proposal, outlining reasons (that is a resumé of those set out above) to all employees setting timetable for implementation (possibly running over six months).

2 Devise suitable wording for a rule to be incorporated in employer's rule-book (or equivalent) and agree it with employees or their representatives.

3 Agree that during run-in period people will be cautioned for smoking but not via the disciplinary procedure. Hence, during this period any cautions issued will be more of the encouragement and counselling than the disciplinary type.

4 Possibly designate a specified area for smoking at least on a temporary basis.

5 Provide counselling support and other assistance to those who decide they wish to use the introduction of such a ban as impetus to give up smoking.

6 Once the introductory phase is complete, monitor the ban more forcefully so that everyone is left in no doubt that the aim is to enforce the rule rigorously.

7 Where there are breaches of the ban post implementation phase, these will need to be dealt with under the disciplinary procedure.

8 Where an employee assistance programme (that is, counselling support) is in operation or where it may be necessary to find a place where confidential counselling can take place, the exclusion of such a room from an otherwise comprehensive ban may be advisable. (A similar exception might usefully be made for rooms where disciplinary hearings take place.)

9 In particular cases it may be helpful, either on an ongoing or short-term basis to set aside a room or place to which smokers can retire occasionally. However, the exact terms of any such 'allowance' must be made clear. Where communication is faulty and/or rules are unclear, only disputes can result.

Case study 13.4
STAMPING IT OUT

When Royal Mail Parcelforce wished to introduce restrictions on smoking it conducted a lengthy and high profile communication project regarding the possibility. Eventually it concluded an agreement with the employees' recognised union – the Union of Communication Workers – that following the introduction of the ban, no formal disciplinary action would be taken against any employee who ignored it during the first six months after the ban. However, once this initial period had expired, the full weight of the ban would come into force and disciplinary action would be taken against offenders.

Key technique
This is such a major and intensely personal change to the whole life of smoking addicts that full implementation of the process will almost inevitably need to be conducted over a long period. The longer time that people are allowed to adjust to such a major change the greater the likelihood of the success of the change.

Case study 13.5
CAUGHT RED-FACED

The employee had been caught smoking in the toilets. There was a handbook rule that smoking was not allowed at the workplace or in the 'no smoking' area in the canteen. However, although there was an unwritten rule that smoking was not allowed in the toilets, such a rule had not previously been enforced and it was generally known that smoking did take place in the toilets. The manager concerned did not like the employee and used the smoking offence as a means to dismiss her.

She appealed and was reinstated. The manager was appalled as it seemed to him that the action undermined his authority. The personnel director pointed out that there was no alternative, as the employee would almost certainly win any tribunal case, since the company could not point to any rule banning what she had done, while she could produce several witnesses to show that smoking in the toilets was condoned.

Key technique
'Turning Nelson's blind eye' may be helpful in certain circumstances, but more often it creates unwanted precedents. Cutting corners or, as here, using one 'offence' as a means of generating sanctions cannot just put the employer in a difficult situation in a tribunal, but has a totally negative spin-off in terms of negative commitment of other employees, who will know that rather than being open and honest, management is resorting to devious methods to gain its aims. This is negative communication.

While, at first consideration, the provision of a 'smoking' room may seem to be an obvious solution to the problem of heavily addicted employees, it can have problem repercussions unless there are rules under which such a room or place can be used. Not only does the number and length of such 'smoking breaks' need to be delineated, and related to the number and length of breaks available to non-smokers, to avoid any backlash against the concession, but also there may need to be set aside a similar 'room' for non-smokers.

Despite every effort being made to assist and a long introductory period being provided some employees will find it impossible to comply with a smoking ban and may then be forced to reconsider their employment. The introduction of such a rule, while it is in many cases a unilateral change to working conditions, will not normally allow an employee to claim constructive dismissal if forced to resign because of such a change. In the *Dryden* v. *Greater Glasgow Health Board* case, a tribunal held that the employee's contract gave her no implied right to smoke at work. The fact that the employer had consulted widely, given reasonable notice of the change, and offered counselling and support to smokers who would be affected stood it in good stead. Sound communication in advance provided an effective defence.

Solvent and drug abuse

In discovering tobacco, Sir Walter Raleigh, himself a fine leader of and communicator with men, has a great deal to answer for, but at least it was one of the problems with which Henry V did not have to cope! However he had others – and so do present day employers. While tobacco may be acceptable in some environments, it is rare for solvent abuse and the use of drugs for non-medicinal purposes to be countenanced. Fortunately the persons affected tend to be a small minority, not that this makes individual problems any less difficult to solve, and in most instances it may be necessary to refer sufferers to experts for assistance – rather than attempting a solution via communication, counselling and so on, internally. Although experts' advice will be invaluable, the employer may have to take the first steps to:

- promulgate a policy stressing the wish of the employer to assist while respecting the rights and confidentiality of the individual;
- recognise the problem for what it is; and
- counsel the employee that he or she needs advice and help.

The Institute of Personnel and Development has issued a booklet 'Substance misuse at work' on this subject.

> ## SUSPECTED ADDICTION SUPPORT CHECKLIST
>
> **1** Identify the symptoms – for example, erratic work, erratic attendance, excited responses to mundane matters, low output and/or quality of work, difficulty interfacing with colleagues, poor attention to appearance, poor health and/or appearance, physical disabilities (running nose, dilated pupils, marked skin etc.).
>
> **2** Attempt to identify the problem. Many of the symptoms described above may indicate addiction, but equally they could indicate a number of other problems. Nothing would be guaranteed to add to the stress of an employee suffering because (say) of the breakdown of a marriage, than to learn that their employer feels they are drug addicted. Someone unable to concentrate on her work, with a running nose and an untidy appearance, could be addicted, but equally these symptoms could be the result of her partner having left her, while she has a persistent, heavy cold.
>
> **3** Don't make assumptions – invite confidence. Rather than setting up an interview and making a statement, invite the person to confide the problem as the symptoms indicate there is a problem with which a responsible employer would like to help if possible and if required.
>
> **4** If the employee refuses to discuss the position, request a medical examination, either by the employer's own retained medical adviser or by the employee's doctor.
>
> **5** If the employee is prepared to identify the problem – take notes without comment and without criticism. Offer access to suitable third party advice or, if apparently welcomed, to personal advice if it is felt that this is of value.
>
> **6** Invite repeated discussions to provide support.
>
> **7** Advise the line manager and possibly colleagues (although this will depend on the problem and the circumstances), stressing the need to provide help and support rather than interference and publicity.
>
> **8** Hold a watching brief, and request further referral to experts as and when necessary.

177

Counselling

Inherent in trying to deal with problems arising from addictions is both a need for as full communication as possible and a need to be able to provide assistance where this is required. Communication in these instances is likely to be even more difficult than normal since the subject may not wish for any interference in what they may regard as their own private affairs. Patient explanation of the impact such problems are having on the business and their colleagues (rather than 'personal prying') is the only way in which the logic of the interest can be explained. Rather than expecting line or personnel managers to try to assist in a well-meaning but possibly amateurish way, it may be preferable to make it known that there is a counselling service whereby external experts are retained to give advice on a range of subjects including addictions. The employer is then seen as the means by which confidential assistance and advice is made available. Once the introduction is made, however, the employee and the expert interface to try to resolve the problem, which may of course be easier said than done.

Employee assistance programmes

Such programmes, which cater for a wide range of problems, not simply addictions, are now operated by around 80 per cent of the top 500 American companies and are becoming increasingly popular in the UK. A survey in 1993 indicated that around 150 UK companies had such programmes and many find them of considerable value in not only helping to solve problems, but also in improving workplace relationships. The programmes are indicative that the employer cares – not just to get the work done, but about the welfare and long-term health (in the widest sense of the word) of its workforce. While the employer sets the programme up and provides information on how advice can be sourced (that is via a comprehensive communication of both problems and suggested alleviation), the rest of the process depends on the employee making the contact and acting on the advice. Ian Anderson, who manages the programme operated by brewers Whitbreads, believes that it has helped improve the efficiency of the employees and encourage a happier workplace. 'If [employees] have problems they will be careless' he stated in an article in the *Financial Times*, 'the programme helps nip problems in the bud'. Such a programme must be given publicity to ensure it is used – 'like any other service, it needs marketing' stated Anderson. Once again effective communication is essential.

14

Dealing with bad news

'We are not interested in the possibilities of defeat'

Key learning points

1 Bad news needs to be communicated as much as good, indeed in such circumstances the 'communication need' may be acute
2 Most employees are well able to deal with news, whether it be good or bad, only resenting not being given the facts straight
3 The application of discipline must be, and be seen to be, fair
4 Employee preferences need to be researched not assumed.

Queen Victoria's comment of 1899 is still relevant nearly 100 years on and should apply to all management at all times. Only if it does will the same commitment to success be shared by their employees. Unless everyone believes in the goal, and believes in themselves and their ability to achieve their goal, nothing will be achieved. Setting achievable targets, telling everyone the progress towards those targets, keeping everyone informed, and sustaining and building morale and involvement, are all essential communication tools as well as being concomitants for ultimate success, even if at the last moment it is taken from you. Speaking just after Manchester had lost its bid to host a future Olympic Games, Sir Bob Scott, chairman of the bid committee, stated 'Manchester had a wonderful nineteenth century, but a pretty moderate twentiethth century . . . we began to look better to the world when we began to think better of ourselves.' We could perhaps paraphrase this by saying that at all times we need to have confidence and belief in ourselves, our ideas and our people. This is relatively easy when things are going well. It is far less easy when things are going badly. It is said that the time finds the man (or woman) and going back to the analogy of the Second World War again, that was certainly true of the UK's leader. Some of Winston Churchill's finest speeches were made when things were at their worst. The ability to rise above such gloom, and to communicate and inspire in such circumstances is, sadly, not given to enough of us, and yet that ability is even more essential when bad events occur or bad news is to be disseminated.

Trade tends to move in cycles of roughly seven and 14 years. By a combination of good judgement and luck, some organisations may be able to evade the worst effects of downturns but, at some time in their existence, most will have periods when things are not going too well. As former chancellor of the exchequer, Nigel Lawson, commented when told of the 1994 UK government's commitment to end the cycle of boom and bust 'the plain fact is that the trade cycle is endemic – which means that the talk of no return to boom and bust is somewhat premature'. While some managements may try to delude themselves into thinking that they can avoid the downturns, most employees are far too canny not to realise that there are bound to be bad times and that, when they come, it will often be them who suffer most through losing their jobs. This can be aggravated by the knowledge that very often this move may have been brought about by poor decisions of those whose jobs are usually protected, but the real aggravation which kills commitment and motivation can be caused if management fails to communicate the bad news in a mature and adult fashion.

180

Censorship – or embarrassment?

In a survey of around 200 members of the British Association of Industrial Editors meeting at their conference in Edinburgh in May 1994 around half confirmed that, at some time or another, they had been prevented from communicating bad news to employees. One would hope that this was merely a timing problem, that is that those responsible for the news blackout merely wished to ensure that the bad news was delayed only so that it could be personally communicated to those affected in a face-to-face manner, which is infinitely better than for those personnel to read about it in a journal, particularly as this might occur in the company of other employees not affected. Unfortunately experience suggests that this is very often not the case and in fact that bad news has a habit of being 'hoarded' so that it eventually 'leaks out'. Alternatively an indication of the bad news is posted as a memo on the organisation's notice boards, thus creating dismay without providing a means by which concerns and questions can be answered.

Case study 14.1
HARDLY THE WAY TO DO IT

An international group with factories and offices throughout the UK was being forced by market conditions to lose a substantial proportion of its workforce. Rumours had been flying around for some time with the only reply when anyone asked for clarification of the situation being 'no comment'. Eventually a memo was posted on most notice boards throughout the group which referred to the organisation being 'downsized'. So obscure was the wording used that many employees did not initially realise that redundancy was being announced. The situation was made immeasurably worse by the fact that not all locations received the memo. So poorly and haphazardly was the announcement made, that union representatives immediately called a strike of the whole workforce, making a difficult situation even worse. This whole episode was aggravated since, under UK personnel legislation, employers are required to negotiate with elected representatives in such situations and the employer here ignored these obligations.

Key technique

- *Apart from the failure to abide by legal requirements, the absence of realisation that those not directly affected by the news would still have a considerable interest (that is confirmation that they still had jobs) in the announcement was inept. One would hardly expect those losing their jobs to have high commitment, but, in such circumstances, the maintenance of morale of those left behind is vital. If they see their erstwhile colleagues poorly treated, they are entitled to assume that that is how they could be treated next time around. 'There but for the grace of God, go I . . .'*

- *The fact that management did not take the initiative that was properly theirs in facing the employees, telling them the news and answering questions, meant that they failed in their main purpose (communicating with and managing people), cost them the initiative in dealing with the situation, and lost them any sympathy in the national press and among their 'continuing' workforce.*

- *Using flowery language to try and avoid 'nasty' words such as redundancy, is patronising in the extreme. It merely adds insult to the injury already being visited on employees.*

181

The situation in case study 14.1 can be contrasted with those in case studies 5.6 and 2.2. In case study 5.6 management had been so frank about the economic situation over a period of years that when the announcement came there was acceptance and understanding rather than aggravation, while in case study 2.2 the constant direct interface with those affected led to record output at a time when most onlookers would have expected there to be very little goodwill. The phrase 'Praise me, scold me but never ignore me' is very relevant in this situation. Most employees are not fools and deserve more than being patronised to the extent that it is felt that they will not be able to 'cope with' bad news. Most employees are perfectly capable of dealing with bad news, what they resent is being patronised, which keeping things quiet, using flowery language and not being frank certainly is.

Not making a drama out of a crisis

When one considers how much time and energy is expended in planning for when things go well (when we have plenty of time to make adjustments to our actions and tactics), it is strange that most organisations spend so little time planning for when things go wrong. Only a small proportion of UK organisations have contingency or disaster plans, even though the benefits of such plans have been proven, particularly in recent years as a result of both natural and 'enemy action' disasters. In the aftermath of such disasters, the one essential ingredient to a swift recovery is the commitment of personnel which will be far more readily provided if it is obvious that management has a clear idea of priorities, tactics and strategies. These can be difficult, if not impossible to develop, let alone communicate if plans are being developed 'on the hoof' rather than outline guidance, already thought out, being refined. The crisis control guidelines set out below should be considered.

Communication guidelines for crisis control

- Prepare a plan (or plans, since there may be several disasters that could 'hit' an organisation). Only the most serious need be addressed, since the plans developed for these tend to be of use for less serious occurrences. (Note: The development of a comprehensive contingency plan lies outside the scope of this book and there are a number of specialists available to help formulate such plans. Only the communication aspects of such a plan are featured here.)

- List requirements – what would you need and who would you need – to act, to liaise and to communicate with. Advance briefing may be needed for key personnel on a 'What if' basis. Involving such personnel and using their ideas can be a valuable communication and commitment exercise in its own right.

- Prepare the ground. From an analysis of these first two points, it is usually the case that immediate action is necessary, even though much may be conditional on the event(s). Such action should be taken.

- Ensure that adequate information trails are set up so that when the disaster strikes, these can be implemented. This may mean briefing or training those people who have to interface with the media, as well as those communicating internally. The two (or more) messages provided need to avoid any possibility of confusion or contradiction. Such communicators should be told to try to tell the truth and, if they do not know an answer, to say so. Better to admit ignorance than to be caught out in a lie. It may also help the communication material gain the respect of the recipients.

- Set up feedback procedures in case this may generate issues needing to be addressed.

183

Attitude

Human beings respond to the situations in which they find themselves and to the attitudes to which they are subject, i.e. we are all conditioned by circumstances.

If we live with criticism, we learn to condemn
If we live with hostility, we learn to fight
If we live with fear, we learn to be apprehensive
But
If we live with encouragement, we learn to be confident
If we live with praise, we learn to be appreciative
If we live with acceptance, we learn to respond.

In attempting to deal with human problems, particularly those which we anticipate we shall encounter when dealing with bad news, we must bear this in mind. Here, as in so many other encounters, the principle of 'Doasyouwouldbedoneby' is all important, while the guidance set out below may be apposite.

Preparing for the encounter

- Have respect for the dignity of the individual (which should also be expected from every employee for the organisation and from fellow employees to each other).

- Anticipate and be prepared for all eventualities and reactions (particularly where it is possible that emotions could run high).

- Back up verbal discussions with written details so that those affected have something to refer to later when calmer and so that some written record exists (this is essential when dealing with disciplinary matters).

- Assess our own reactions were we to be placed in the same position and have to deal with the questions posed or criticism levied.

- Try to second-guess all the questions that could be asked, and answer them, preferably in writing, so that the subject can consider them after any face-to-face interview.

Case study 14.2
PREPARATION WINS THROUGH

The company had been hit by the recession and it was obvious that productive capacity, despite all efforts, would exceed demand for some time to come. It was decided to cut the production workforce on a 'last in, first out basis' by around 30 per cent and it was also decided that to effect this the managing director (supported by the production director and personnel consultant) would address the whole production workforce, explaining the problem and the proposed solution. Questions would be invited, but it would be explained that those selected for redundancy on the basis stated would be seen individually following the general meeting by one of the directors and each would be given a letter setting out their individual circumstances and payments. Although there were 60 people who had to be made redundant, within an hour of the general meeting, all had been seen individually by a director, had been given a statement of their personal position, and had had an opportunity to discuss their immediate reactions and concerns, and an invitation to repeat the personal interview and/or counselling when they had had time to appreciate the decision.

Key technique
Considerable thought had been given to the timing of and the way in which the news was communicated to both those that would go and those that would stay. The meeting was fixed for a Friday afternoon and once the meetings had been held work was suspended, and the employees were encouraged to return home, taking with them their individual letters confirming their own position. Thus they could, at least initially, discuss their position with their families and without immediate input (which might become somewhat emotive) from their colleagues.

There were no problems with the whole process – indeed some jobs were saved as other employees volunteered for redundancy. During the process a number of employees (including both those who had been made redundant and those who were staying), some of whom had been made redundant previously, complimented the company on the way in which the process had been handled. That the process should be handled in such a way was felt to be vital not just because that was the company's philosophy and it wished to be regarded in a good light by the remaining workforce, but primarily because it fully appreciated that being made redundant is a very debilitating and ego-shattering process. Trying to effect redundancy painlessly is impossible, but it can be done humanely and with respect for the individuals affected and their personal positions.

Case study 14.3
THANK YOU FOR TELLING ME

Before the decision was taken to withdraw from its CTN retailing business, Maynards had tried a number of other options, including the closure of its warehouses. In closing the Bristol warehouse, the company prepared individual information (in the same way as the company in case study 14.2) and, on a bleak day in November, three directors journeyed to Bristol to break the news to the staff. While it came as shock, the fact that they had been told face to face was appreciated, some of the staff even thanking the directors for the way it was done and two expressing sympathy for the directors having to do such a 'nasty job'.

Key technique
Ducking the nasty encounters wins no medals or commitment. Facing up to it may actually gain commitment and not only from those who are left. It is never pleasant, but those in control have a duty to tell those affected face to face – that is the responsibility of a communicative management.

Sadly some managers view redundancy in the same light as dismissal, regarding those leaving as having in some way failed the company. Where this attitude exists it is essential that it is corrected. In the company cited in case study 14.2, one director had this view until it was pointed out forcibly by the personnel consultant, that far from the employees having let the company down, it was the company, of which controlling and directing board he was a member, that had let the employees down. Poor decisions made by the board, who were keeping their jobs, were being paid for by 60 employees losing theirs.

Redundancy alternatives

It should not be overlooked that there are other alternatives to removing labour costs than making part of the workforce redundant and often, when given the choice, employees make what an outsider may feel is a surprising choice and decide to maintain the headcount but to take a pay cut. Such a decision can only be made by the workforce itself, but aptly demonstrates that one cannot afford to assume people's reactions. Far better to take time to discover and communicate all the facts, and to encourage people to make their views known – and to listen to what can be valuable suggestions.

Case study 14.4
MOTIVATING IN A COLD CLIMATE

Writing in *Personnel Management* in June 1994, human resource director of Midland Electricity, Clive Parsons recounted the instance when staff costs needed to be cut in the company's fringe contracting business. The choice offered was either a paycut of around 20 per cent over three years or for the company to quit the business altogether. A roadshow was launched for employees, giving facts and details of the choice, and as a result the employees voted two to one in favour of the pay cut.

Key technique
The company granted choice to their workforce over their own destiny. Basically, at a time when many businesses were collapsing and over 3,000,000 were unemployed, the Midland Electricity staff had the option of lower wages or redundancy. Their choice may have been limited, but at least they were consulted. Communication and consultation may lead to commitment; lack of either never can.

In the same article, the following four points for boosting employee commitment were listed:

- success of the organisation, because people like to be associated with success;
- creation of meaningful and fulfilling jobs;
- opportunity for employees to improve their skills; and
- positive caring leadership.

Passing the buck

The antithesis of positive communicating leadership, referred to previously in this book and exemplified by the management in case studies 14.2 and 14.3, is surrendering to the temptation to 'blame the employees' for matters which are properly the responsibility of the board. Sadly this attitude of 'find someone to blame' is far more widespread than is generally realised and is very much a British disease, inextricably linked to our being far too ready to criticise and far too unwilling to provide praise.

Case study 14.5
WHOSE RESPONSIBILITY?

The food factory was in a poor way. For some years little had been spent on its fabric. Each departmental team was responsible for cleaning their own area, but their manual efforts were gradually being overtaken by years of accumulated grime and deteriorating surfaces. Output was also a problem and morale was low. To combat all three problems the factory director decided to introduce a 'clean room competition' with a trophy and cash prize to be presented each month to the department with the cleanest area. The personnel director stated flatly that she was totally against such a scheme. Since she was normally a firm supporter of such incentive and reward schemes the factory director was nonplussed.

'I have no real problem with the idea of the scheme, indeed I feel in other circumstances it could help morale and thus output, but it is completely wrong to expect the employees to try and overcome our lack of commitment to the fabric of the building. We need to invest in a proper professional clean and refurbishment of the building first, putting it into good order, and then challenge the employees with the competition to keep it that way. Cleaning is poor currently because the employees face an impossible challenge due to the company's persistent lack of investment.'

Key technique
Research indicates that if an area is tidy and a bin for rubbish is placed conveniently, it tends to stay tidy. If it is untidy to begin with, it will remain so and tend to become even less tidy. Trying to overcome years of neglect, the responsibility of someone else, by encouraging others to contribute their work and efforts is likely to be demotivational, and to create resentment rather than commitment.

Following an extensive refurbishment of the factory, cleaning standards rapidly improved – with many teams becoming totally committed to the cleanliness and tidiness of their areas. Not only were the teams aware that their cleaning efforts were effective, but also their commitment was enhanced as it was obvious that the company also cared because it was prepared to invest in the factory. By its actions a number of messages had been communicated by the company in a far more effective manner than any briefing or poster campaign.

Discipline

All organisations have rules and wish those involved to work in accordance with those rules. Most people readily accept the fact that there must be rules and that they must be complied with. Of the cases that finish in tribunals seldom are employers' rules themselves criticised, but often cases are lost simply because employers fail to abide by their own rules. It is this that aggravates employees and destroys motivation. Many employees prefer managers who are strict and fair to those who are less strict but inconsistent – at least, runs their attitude, one knows where one is with the former. To ensure motivation it is essential to have an adequate disciplinary process and to ensure strict compliance with it.

Disciplinary system

The primary purpose of a disciplinary procedure should always be to attempt to display, to the 'offending' employee, the nature of the transgression, with the aim of converting unacceptable behaviour to that acceptable to the organisation (rather than the means to obtain evidence that will support a dismissal and win any potential tribunal case).

Such a system must be:

- recognisable, in that the methods by which warnings are given and progressed to more serious levels and more senior levels of management for action, are clearly laid down;
- fair, in that at all times during the application of the procedure, the views of and explanations by both parties are put to, listened to and taken account of by the other side, and decisions are only made, after consideration of such representations;

- accepted, in that the procedure, by being seen to be both recognisable and fair, is accepted by both management and employees as a necessary part of the process of managing and working for the company;
- adhered to at all times, possibly being overseen by one central person to ensure consistency.

Most disciplinary matters can be dealt with informally at the workplace by the immediate superior – chargehand, supervisor or manager. This will comprise a few – friendly or otherwise – words putting the employee 'straight' on a transgression, or inappropriate attitude or action. Such actions may not be thought of as part of a disciplinary procedure or even part of a communication process, but this kind of informal 'nudge back into line', can be far more effective in terms of creating an awareness of the exact type of behaviour required, without the trappings of formality. If, however, such informal 'nudges' need constant repeating, obviously the more formal part of the disciplinary process needs to be invoked, not just to deal with the offender but to ensure fairness towards other employees. Unfairness destroys motivation.

189

Takeover

By far the most challenging 'bad news' scenario in ensuring that employees are kept motivated and committed occurs when control of the employing organisation is undergoing change, either through takeover or merger. Unfortunately often the requirements for confidentiality and control over the dissemination of information inherent in such a process are diametrically opposed to the preference for full disclosure. Strangely enough there can actually be a benefit (at least in the short term) to the organisation when its own existence is threatened.

Case study 14.6
OH NO YOU DON'T, SUNSHINE!

Five days before Christmas, the predator launched a takeover bid for the public company. Little was known of the predator and less was liked. The predator's plans, should the bid succeed, would have led to the break up and sale of parts of the group. The bid was labelled 'opportunistic and unwelcome' by the defending board which, throughout the nine weeks that the bid was fought, sought at all times to keep all its employees aware of what was going on, although detail was kept short due to the requirements of the Takeover Panel which oversees the conduct of such bids.

The attitude of the employees was fascinating. While a minority were somewhat fatalistic and resigned themselves to ultimately being out of work, the majority were outraged at the bid and demanded to know what they could do to help defeat it. The advice of the board to work as normally as possible and not to discuss details of the company's operations outside was noted, but output during the period rose perceptibly, inter-department rivalries and arguments all but disappeared, people worked more willingly and generally the whole workforce became much more closely bound and committed to their targets, and to the preservation of the status quo.

Information concerning the predator was sought by some employees and passed through to the board, and an informal publicity machine (supplementing the official source) was in operation through which employees let their views be known to press, local and national government, and so on.

Key technique
As noted in Chapter 1, the imposition of an external threat can have the effect of removing any blurred aims and restoring priorities – in this case the defeat of what was regarded as a totally unsuitable outsider, which was eventually accomplished.

15

Internal assistance

'You stand like greyhounds in the slips, straining upon the start'

Key learning points

1 Employees' contribution to the success of the employer can be a means of effective communication as well as a means of generating additional profit
2 Checking employees' attitudes can be beneficial but needs to be conducted with care
3 Delegating and empowering must start from the top
4 Leaders must lead and communicate in order to motivate.

Suggestion schemes

Suggestion schemes work on the premise that no one should understand the job in hand better than the person actually performing it, and that their ideas are valuable. Although improving profitability and/or productivity and efficiency or saving money are quantifiable effects of operating such a scheme, it is probable that of greater value is the motivational force created by employees' discussing work-related issues and ideas for improvements (that is undertaking a straightforward communication project), and then seeing their ideas benefiting the business. Some ideas will be trivial and implemented instantly and without much thought, nevertheless all such additions to profitability (tiny or not) mount up. It is essential that all ideas are recognised in some way, not just to acknowledge the thought of the originator but also to encourage others to contribute.

Recently an increasing number of businesses have introduced, or reintroduced, such schemes, some of which have been linked with productivity reward schemes. The Industrial Society estimated recently that there are between 400 and 500 schemes in operation, and in its own survey of 103 schemes, noted that over 73,000 suggestions had been received, or roughly five from every 100 employees, while around 20 per cent had been taken up.

Case study 15.1
RICHER BY FAR

Richer Sounds is a 70-employee, £12 million turnover company that readily acknowledges that it receives many of its best ideas from its staff. Examples include a discount scheme which boosted sales tenfold and a policy of telephoning customers to check that they were happy with a repair service. The company funds monthly brainstorming sessions for employees in pubs local to the company's 12 stores. The number of suggestions made by each store count towards a competition won by the store with most suggestions. All suggestions, whether accepted or not, are rewarded by the company. The rewards range from £5 to a trip on the Orient Express.

Key technique
The employer is using the scheme not just to generate ideas to help improve profits, but also as a social event and a means of generating some competitive spirit, both of which help to bind individuals into teams and the company.

From the author's How to Control your Costs and Increase your Profits, *Directors Books 1992.*

Case study 15.2
INFLATING THE PROFITS

An employee at Dunlop General Rubber Products in Manchester suggested, via the company's 'Bright Spark' suggestion scheme, a change to the way the company cut the foam rubber used in vehicle mats. The suggestion reduced waste and saved the company £7,500 a year. Another employee suggested a new method of removing the blemishes from rubber products which saved the company over £12,000, part of the £54,000 saved in one year alone by the company from ideas generated by the company's scheme.

Key technique
The value of these two suggestions may be somewhat larger than the average, but all, large or small, add to the profits. Dunlop gives a corporate pen to every contributor as well as a mug bearing the slogan 'I am a Dunlop Bright Spark' to those whose ideas are taken up.

Case study 15.3
INVESTING IN PEOPLE PAYS OFF

As part of its commitment to the Investors in People initiative, Land-Rover, when faced with increased worldwide competition, asked its employees for ideas. In the first year of its existence the company's new suggestion scheme generated 15,000 suggestions, improved output by 33 per cent, productivity by 25 per cent and saved over £1,600,000.

The rewards outlined above are not generated simply by announcing that there is a suggestion scheme to all employees. The scheme itself must be introduced carefully and promoted consistently, as follows.

- Plan the whole scheme carefully – ensuring that as many employees as possible are eligible. Almost inevitably it will be necessary to exclude those involved in research and development (part of whose responsibilities will normally include generating new ideas), as well as those involved in production study, organisation and methods, and anyone with similar duties.

- Appoint a senior manager to take responsibility for introducing and running the scheme. With a large workforce the time requirements should not be underestimated. The fact that a senior person is involved will provide an indication that top management are committed to the concept.

- Set up a judging panel which should appear objective and impartial. Representatives of employees should sit on such a panel with possibly a non-executive director or someone not directly connected with the organisation. No one connected with the judging panel should be able to make a suggestion. This may mitigate against employees participating in the panel, although to preserve this option, which helps justice to be seen to be done as well as being done, 'terms of office' could be kept short.

- Rewards should be paid. The average seems to be about a fifth of the value of the idea. It may be helpful for each idea adopted to set a useful life (restricted to a period no longer than, say, three years) and pay out a proportion of the value each year. In this way the successful 'suggester', as well as his or her colleagues, will be reminded of the value of the scheme.

- The paperwork should be kept as simple as possible.

Case study 15.4
FIRST SUGGESTION – STREAMLINE THE SCHEME!

The paperwork for the suggestion scheme was complex – the forms took up four pages – and because of the nature of the business, some suggestions could not be outlined within the layout of the forms provided. On receiving a set of the forms, the employee worked out that in an average year and assuming one-fifth of the employees made one suggestion each, over 4,000 sheets of paper would be used, much of it wasted, while the time involved in ploughing through such complexities could exceed a working year for one employee! Instead of making his original suggestion he recommended a much simpler way of recording suggestions. His idea was accepted and an award made!

Key technique
It should be remembered that those who will complete the forms may not be used to dealing with written material, so any forms should be kept as simple as possible. Indeed, simply requiring completion of complex forms will almost certainly mean that the number of suggestions may be severely reduced. The value of any suggestion made is usually determinable, however poorly it is described. Where there is potential, the scheme administrator can work with the 'suggester' to originate a full version.

- Confidentiality should be preserved to minimise the possibility of 'poaching' of ideas. This can be effected by the suggestions being handed in sealed envelopes to the administrator and a receipt bearing a rough guide to the idea being given to the 'suggester'. This should bear the date that the idea was presented. It should not be overlooked that the person making the suggestion may gain 'rights' to the suggestion and adequate protection of such rights needs to be provided.

Case study 15.5
DANGER – ESCAPING IDEAS

An employee of British Gas designed and built a few prototypes of a device aimed to reduce vandalism to roadwork lamps. He decided to patent the device although British Gas had decided not to use it, even though they paid him for it. However it was discovered that British Gas had used the prototypes publicly and had disclosed information about them to a third party. In a subsequent case, it was held that British Gas had an obligation to keep the details confidential.

Key technique
How suggestions can be used and where the rights to such suggestions lie
should be addressed in the scheme rules, and the point clearly communicated to all involved.

- All ideas should be given an initial consideration and a likely decision (that is acceptance or not) within two weeks. Leaving the consideration time longer than this mitigates against employees' continuing interest.

- The scheme should be given constant and original publicity, and, whenever an award is made, photos should be taken and promoted widely.

195

- The success of the scheme depends on the commitment of the workforce to the concept. As such, rather like the idea of the house newspaper, the whole scheme must have an element of fun or at least of being enjoyable. The promotion material should stress this aspect without trivialising the point in any way.

- As well as individual awards it may be helpful to award an additional 'star prize' to the most valuable suggestion in a year. If the value of individual suggestions is not thought likely to amount to a great deal, it may be advisable to make this subject to either the total exceeding a set figure or to an individual suggestion exceeding that figure. However, the purpose of the star prize is to aid promotion and hedging it with too many provisos is the surest way to demotivate the very people you want to motivate.

Suggestion schemes can be valuable means of supporting a comprehensive communication process, as well as a means of generating extra profits and employee commitment. They cannot perform such tasks on their own, and there is a need for a genuine communications policy and practice to be in place first to ensure the success of the scheme. Without this some schemes, despite every appearance of being successful, fail miserably. While the mechanics may be correct, the attitude of the target audience is wrong.

Attitude surveys

Gauging the attitude of the workforce is an undertaking which can be effective as a means of discovering some general trends or views, but great care needs to be taken in setting up the investigation and analysing the results. The research quoted here from MORI and other organisations has the benefit of being drawn from a wide selection of industries and employers, and from a large number of individuals. In addition, those selected to answer the questions knew the research organisations and their reputations. Even then providing answers to a list of questions may not obtain the objective answers which are sought.

Case study 15.6
YOU'RE NOT CATCHING ME OUT LIKE THAT

The company wished to proceed with a sizeable redundancy programme, and to try and provide it with an indication of the flexibility of its workforce required employees to answer a questionnaire which included questions such as:

- Would you be prepared to relocate 25, 50 or 100 miles or more?

- How committed are you to the area, schools, in which you live?

- How great are your family ties in the area in which you live?

- Are you averse to travelling to work 10, 20 or more miles? and so on.

The information, if obtained objectively and truthfully, could have helped plan a reorganisation, except that the employees swiftly realised if they told the truth at that stage they could be putting themselves on an initial redundancy list and thus many of the answers received did not reflect their real attitudes or preferences, but rather those that they felt might preserve their jobs as long as possible!

Key technique
This highlights the whole problem with written response attitude surveys. The same problem is encountered to a lesser effect with face-to-face surveys – as we saw with Joe's devious mind in case study 3.4. Faced with a questionnaire, as well as the questions posed on the paper, the recipient receives a further semiotic or hidden message – someone wants my opinion. This awareness and the perception of the reasons for the request can immediately condition the response.

This is widely recognised by companies carrying out such surveys. Research Services Ltd, one of the top five UK market research companies, states that it is important to 'bury' the main subject of the questionnaire among more general questions so that any 'hothouse' effect is offset. In addition, the compilers of questionnaires try to compensate for the fact that respondents do manufacture their answers by inserting 'camouflage' questions which, because a lie is more difficult to remember than the truth, may be answered differently, indicating that the answer to the original question may be suspect.

This is not to say that attitude surveys do not have a part to play, but simply that there needs to be some caution in considering the answers generated. In seeking opinions as part of a communication process, the very act indicates an implied message, which is that the status quo will change. This raises expectations. Some employees asked for their comments may feel flattered and encouraged to answer accurately. However, others, particularly those with an axe to grind, may skew their replies to try to generate action. Both are conditioned to expect change. If change does not then occur, their subsequent reaction, and resentment, will create a negative commitment and a worse situation than was originally the case.

197

Case study 15.7
WHY DID YOU BOTHER TO ASK?

The company felt it had a communication problem and sent out a short questionnaire to all its employees, asking them to rank in order of preference five means by which internal communication could be improved. The means suggested were:

- company house journal;
- cascade briefing;
- regular formal meetings;
- monthly management updates;
- greater dissemination of information using electronic mail facility (virtually all the employees had access to a computer).

While many did rank and return the questionnaire, there was an orchestrated effort to 'write in' a further alternative – that of regular briefings by the, very popular, managing director.

The managing director was a shy person who, though he did not realise it, was actually a very effective communicator. Unfortunately he was also extremely committed and there was no way in which he felt he could undertake the briefings suggested. The outcome was that nothing was done. Six months later, when a consultant was asked to survey the staff to gain their views on how communication could be improved, he had a very difficult time trying to gain any positive response, mainly because the employees felt that their previous views and preferences had been ignored.

Key technique
Unless you intend doing something, don't ask! Once you have asked you have raised expectations and if such anticipation of improvement is then disappointed, the resulting attitude problems will be worse than they were originally.

198

SARAH

Anyone seeking to learn attitudes, and everyone who has to interface with people, may need guidance and assistance to ensure they can perform this essential task well. It is probably true that the best communicators and leaders are born, but all of us can improve – and if we aim to be great communicators it is vital that we do. There can never be any question of resting on one's laurels. As already stressed, good communication requires an ongoing and consistent commitment.

The principles of good direct communication and interfacing can be summed up in the process described by the mnemonic SARAH. SARAH is a friendly and helpful export from the USA and, although she was originated for use more in selling, her principles apply equally to employee relationships:

- **s**mile and stop talking;
- **a**ctive listening;
- **r**epetition of content;
- **a**ct with empathy; and
- **h**andle the subject matter with appreciation of employees' feelings.

Smile and stop talking

If the manager is talking the employee cannot be heard and neither can their views, suggestions or concerns. Nothing riles people more than for the other party to keep talking, preventing them putting their point. It seems that an attempt is being made to 'talk out' the subject matter. Smiling (particularly by a superior) relaxes most employees and may encourage them to 'open up'.

Case study 15.8
KEEP SMILING SIR!

As a little bit of fun for inclusion in the company newspaper at Christmas, the editor invited employees to send in their favourite memories of the year. Out of 20 or so that were received, three referred to 'the managing director's smile'. The editor was intrigued and in general conversation with one of those who had mentioned this brought the chat round to the managing director. He discovered that when they saw the MD smile, the staff felt that everything was fine and felt that they could talk to him – but when he was not smiling, they kept out of his way as 'things' were obviously not going so well.

Key technique
This is another example of the hidden messages we communicate by our body language. No doubt often, when he was not smiling, the MD may have been preoccupied with other matters – not even necessarily work-related, but the impression in a small, tightly-knit company was that unless the MD was smiling the staff felt they did not wish to approach him. In such circumstances, communication and motivation cannot take place. In view of the small numbers involved one would expect communication where few people are employed to be most effective, but MORI found in its 1994 survey that organisations employing fewer than 100 people were actually the least effective communicators.

199

Even with communication encounters where the parties cannot see each other, the value of a smile should not be overlooked. Using computers for personal communication with instant transmission of one's thoughts can be dangerous. To offset any unintended misunderstandings or over hasty responses, those using electronic transmission (E-mail) of memos, notes, letters, etc., sometimes type in a 'smilie'. A smilie is made up of the colon, dash and closing bracket, thus :-) which, if you turn the book through 90 degrees should resemble a smiling face. In addition, the effect of a really outrageous comment might be offset by the use of a 'winkie' (period, dash and closing bracket) thus .–). Of course there is nothing to stop such a device being used in ordinary correspondence!

Active listening

The corollary to ceasing to talk is to listen more. This means much more than hearing what is said, as indicated earlier. Hearing is purely a mechanical act, whereas listening entails active consideration of what is both said and left unsaid, bearing in mind that the speaker may be saying what he or she thinks their manager wants to hear. Only if we listen constantly will we gain the real views of the other party. The longer employees talk the more they reveal of their true feelings. In addition the longer they are allowed to talk and believe that the discussion will achieve some results, the greater should be their commitment. Most people want to be involved, and to feel that their views count and can assist. This is the theory behind employee empowerment.

Case study 15.9
I AM EMPOWERED THEREFORE I ACT

In an article in the December 1993 edition of the Industrial Society's monthly newsletter *Briefing Plus*, a supervisor at Buckingham Foods was quoted as follows:

> I used to come in and pick up a sheet which said how many sandwiches we had to produce and what variety. I had no influence on the number of staff, how long the process should take, or any direct control over the machinery. But now if the line breaks down, I don't just report it to my superior. I have the authority to get hold of the engineer. I have production targets and I want to meet them.

Key technique
By thrusting authority down and making employees accountable, the emphasis is changed from 'must' meet the targets to 'want' to meet the targets. The person is involved, and from such involvement is derived commitment and motivation.

Repetition of content

To show that the manager has understood what the employee has said they should repeat key sentences or comments in their own words. This has four advantages:

- it helps fix the details of the problem in the mind of the manager;
- it helps check that what has been received by the manager was what was meant by the employee;
- it engenders a rapport and understanding between the two, again leading to greater commitment and motivation; and
- it leads to real accurate communication.

Case study 15.10
WHOSE OBLIGATION TO CLARIFY?

One of the responsibilities of the new production manager was to interface with the union representatives. Previously industrial relations had been very harmonious and a spirit of 'constructive compromise' had usually overcome difficulties. Within a short space of time this disintegrated and the personnel director investigated. She found that in place of the previous rapport between manager and chief shop steward, there was now considerable enmity. Sitting in on a routine discussion, she realised that the shop steward was inarticulate and found it difficult to express himself. Whereas his predecessor had possessed the patience to assist the steward to put his feelings into the appropriate words, the present manager had no such patience and was dismissive of the steward's attempts to express himself.

Key technique
Many employees suffer from this problem. The onus, in the interest of good communication and motivation, is then on the management to assist. Ignoring or, far worse, ridiculing the problem serves merely to aggravate and destroy rapport. It may seek to enhance the status of the respondent, but this is likely to be a cheap and short-lived victory.

201

Act with empathy

This entails showing that management understands and appreciates the feelings and motivation of the employee(s). If empathy and perception are lacking, employees will conclude that they are wasting their time as the organisation does not really care about their views. Conversely, if management is seen to have listened and then to have acted, even if only partially, in the way required by the employee, again commitment and motivation is likely to be achieved.

Handle the subject matter with appreciation of employees' feelings

Most employee concerns revolve around their position and security. To each employee these are real problems and, although most will appreciate that it is impossible for management to answer all such questions, limited reassurance will always be valued and generate commitment.

Delegation and empowerment

It is estimated that half the employees in the average organisation are capable of performing more demanding responsibilities than those they currently have. This is a considerable waste of talent, as well as being a waste of the wages or salaries given to such employees. Unleashing such capacity is an important method of improving communication, and gaining motivation and commitment, simply because to implement it, the two parties need to talk and discuss matters. This is not a question of management abdicating its responsibilities, but of positive delegation thereby freeing itself to plan for the future, to manage and motivate, and to be available for coaching and guidance.

Delegation which involves complete and ongoing communication should be practised widely at all levels in order to maximise the investment in people. This is not to say that subordinates should simply have duties loaded on to them – delegation or, as it is currently known, empowerment, needs to be structured, monitored and assessed. The principles of delegation are as follows:

Principles of delegation

- assess the subordinate for capability and willingness to assume a greater workload;

- establish precisely the duties, responsibilities and authority that are to be delegated;

- consider whether the subordinate can assume extra duties delineated immediately, or needs training or a delay before taking over such duties;

- delegate only to those able to carry out the work;

- brief and train the delegatee to carry out the work;

- advise all involved of the delegation;

- provide time, support and guidance for the delegatee;

- avoid the destruction of confidence by undercutting the authority of the delegatee;

- regularly review progress and accomplishments;

- motivate rather than denigrate.

The benefits can be very real. Writing in the journal of the Institute of Personnel and Development, Tony Miller, of Frizzell Financial Services, claimed that his organisation had saved £250,000 through empowered teamworking.

203

Middle management under threat

However, such benefits, financial or in improved commitment terms, are often not as effective as they might otherwise be simply because middle management is apathetic towards or even downright obstructive regarding its implementation. Thus, winning the hearts and minds of such people is vital to ensure its success. In a survey carried out by consultants Harbridge House, it was disclosed that no less than 62 per cent of organisations stated that their middle managers felt insecure in some way or other regarding the process, and that as a result they were unwilling to 'let go' and fearful of the change. Such a reaction cannot simply be ignored or such managers be forced to accept a new method of working – since unless we believe in something we cannot commit to it. Inevitably communication cannot be present in such circumstances.

Case study 15.11
BUT WHAT DO THEY DO?

I was recently asked by an acquaintance, a supervisor working for one of the UK's largest companies, what managers are supposed to do? I asked the reason for the question. 'Well ours don't do anything except sit in their offices – we hardly ever see them.' The reality may not have been as bald as the statement – no doubt the managers were working – but they were hardly managing and they certainly were not communicating.

I commented that they should be communicating, motivating and leading their teams to achieve the targets for their department, and, unless they were, it was difficult to understand how they expected their employees to work effectively. 'They don't' came the answer. 'Everyone does the least they can get away with.'

Key technique
If managers do not manage, lead, motivate and communicate, why should employees work, other than when prompted by their own self-respect? The need for directors, managers and supervisors to become great communicators is not just a 'good thing', it is essential for the success (or greater success) of the organisation.

The challenge is to convince middle managers that communication techniques such as empowerment are effective tools – both for the company and for them. The evidence is available. After all 40 per cent of respondents to the survey stated that it 'increased the motivation, commitment, energy and enthusiasm of the workforce', while over 33 per cent thought it improved 'customer focus, increased job enrichment and a sense of ownership', and 20 per cent stated that it reduced labour turnover.

But throwing statistics at people is no way to win their minds and commitment, and in this respect the wheel comes full circle. If we wish to empower those at the sharp end, we delegate powers from first line management. To empower first line management we should be delegating power and responsibility from middle management, and to empower middle management we need to delegate power and responsibility from top management. We are back to Henry V, and Eisenhower and Montgomery, and the need for top level leadership and communication. There is little point in top management telling middle management to delegate, communicate with and empower their subordinates, unless they are prepared to do the same. Indeed *only* if the process starts at the top can it be effective at all. Unless top management are great communicators it is difficult to envisage how their subordinates can be such – other than in a limited way.

'You never have so much authority as when you give it away'

It is said that there is no such thing as bad men, only bad leaders. At a conference on radical change in 1994, a number of top managers blamed their organisations' inflexibility and inadequacies on the 'mushy middle' (management). Apart from being another example of the British disease of finding someone to blame, the contention is entirely false. After all, who appointed the 'mushy middle' to their positions – and who have the power to remove them? *'Qui s'excuse, s'accuse'* – if middle management is not doing its job, it can be replaced, but if top management is not doing its job – what then? The job in this respect is managing as well as communicating – although the two are to a great extent indistinguishable.

205

16

The external dimensions

'Peace treaty'

> **Key learning points**
>
> 1 Internal communications can have considerable repercussions externally
> 2 Only if employees are communicated with positively will they (usually the actual contact point with the customers of the organisation) be encouraged to become great communicators
> 3 Communicating effectively (and investing in the process) generates benefits in the most unlikely ways
> 4 The message, the medium, the target audience – and their likely reaction - all need to be considered carefully.

The aim of this book has been to explore ways in which we can achieve the aim of being a great communicator, or at least become more adept and successful at the task. Essentially this has been examined from the internal perspective. But, as highlighted in case study 16.1, there is a further equally or even more important dimension, namely that of communicating externally – with our customers without whom we do not have a business and cannot retain employees.

> **Case study 16.1**
> **SMILING'S ADDITIONAL DIMENSION**
>
> It is not only internally that smiling and smiles (see case study 15.8) can be used as incentives and criteria. In a national advertising campaign in late 1994, the airline Lufthansa announced, having recited some of its accomplishments over a 40-year period that 'our most important objective remains unchanged. Your smile.'

Key technique

If we can generate smiles both internally and externally then perhaps not only are we succeeding in our aims, particularly with our customers, but also we are moving a very long way towards being a great communicator in both dimensions. It is unlikely that the organisation can generate smiles from its satisfied customers, unless the organisation's own internal customers (its employees) are themselves smiling.

Case study 16.2
SMILE, SMILE, SMILE

An article in the *Financial Times* in October 1993 illustrated the value of encouraging employees to smile and to be welcoming to customers. Harrington Caravans, based in the Delamere Forest in Cheshire, believe that a customer's first impressions of a company are all-important and encourage all their employees to greet customers with a smile and a 'good morning'. Similarly, the former owner of a garden centre in Chester-le-Street, County Durham, insisted that his staff, despite the fact that their tasks often required them to look down in tending plants and so on, should look up and greet customers. Echoing comments repeatedly made here and in particular the philosophies exemplified in case studies 3.6 and 3.7, regular *FT* columnist Charles Batchelor commented 'the benefits of these efforts should come in loyal customers, who, over the years will spend large sums with the company. Existing customers are far easier and cheaper to reach than new ones, whilst satisfied customers will promote the company for free. Dissatisfied customers, in contrast, talk to far more people' – hell hath no fury like a dissatisfied customer.

Case study 16.3
SERVICE IS OUR FORTE

Our staff can only satisfy our customers if they themselves are satisfied. To achieve processes of delegation, empowerment, quality management and so forth can be employed. Whatever name it is given, or whatever process is used, the common thread in achieving all is adequate communication between management and front line employees. As Rocco Forte, chief executive of the Forte Hotel group, commented in a 1994 television advert 'At the end of the day what makes one hotel better than the other is the people in it. It doesn't matter how clever you are at the top if you're not delivering the detail at the bottom.'

Similarly, Sir Iain Vallance, Chairman of British Telecom, writing in the Institute of Personnel and Development's journal in September 1994 commented 'after all it is people who give a company competitive advantage, more than state of the art technology and much more than robust legal, finance and accounting systems . . . it is the virtues of responsiveness, understanding, commitment to customers and the ability to learn as an organisation that will increasingly distinguish the most successful companies from the rest. The most important factor in determining which companies come out as winners is the human factor.'

Key technique

Dealing with customers successfully is the subject of one of my earlier books in this series (Dealing With Demanding Customers, Pitman Publishing, 1994) and in discussing communication internally it is essential that the link between these essential in-house communications and the effect they should have on external communications is recognised. If employees receive the information they need, and are allowed to communicate and to make suggestions, and to become involved in the aims and execution of their employer's organisation, this will be evidenced in the way that they deal with the customers of that organisation.

208

An apathetic and uncommitted workforce can only ever provide a neutral or even negative attitude to the customers – in turn this will either reduce the orders won by (or sales generated by) the organisation or actually lose orders. Those at the sharp end are often the only point of contact with the customer. What they say and how they say it is vital to the success of every business.

Case study 16.4
POOR VISION

The print on packaging becoming ever smaller, I needed spectacles but dislike carrying expensive glasses when out shopping. An advertisement for folding glasses seemed to solve the problem and I telephoned an order, paying by credit card. Nothing was heard for eight weeks, although the amount had been debited from my credit card.

On telephoning the company, the bored voice of a young girl mumbled the question 'Was the magnification 3 dioptres?' I confirmed this was so, and was then told that in that case they were still awaiting delivery which was expected 'very soon'. I enquired in that case why they had debited my account six weeks previously. 'That's for security – we can't leave cheques lying around here.' 'But this is an Access debit.' Silence. Since at this point not a single word of apology for the delay had been offered I cancelled the order. Even in doing that, 'bored voice' had to be reminded that, as well as my name and address, they would want the Access account details in order to refund the amount taken.

Result

One lost order, one set of costs with no revenue, one dissatisfied customer and one potentially adverse public relations sore.

'Bored voice' should not be criticised out of hand as perhaps she had received neither training, direction nor effective communication from her employer, which would have shown her how to handle such an encounter positively. If she had, it is difficult to believe that her performance was being monitored by supervision. In either case better communication would have avoided this lost sale. Her managing director was horrified at the news of her response and stated that that was not the way in which the company expected customer response to operate. He was obviously aware of the need for positive customer communication, but it seemed that the internal communication of his requirements was faulty.

209

Communicate to survive

As Sir John Harvey Jones comments in *Managing to Survive* (Collins 1993) 'I believe the 90s are going to punish those who do not think fundamentally about [their] problems.' If we need to become better at what we are doing in order to survive, communicating with our employees so that they in turn can communicate effectively with customers (i.e. become great communicators in their own right), is vital. Such communication is not only essential in face-to-face (or voice-to-voice) contacts.

Case study 16.5
SLOW SERVICE

In 1992, on behalf of the *Sunday Times*, a correspondent wrote to 65 leading UK companies and public bodies. 'Full replies came back in anything from three to 49 days and varied from prompt, charming and informative to late, curt and rude. Nine have yet to write back despite a reminder.'

Key techniques
- *In the article, Vincent Mitchell, lecturer in marketing at the University of Manchester, stated that the way an organisation deals with its correspondence reveals a lot about how it is run. 'How they reply is indicative of the way they view their marketplace, and an indication of the philosophy of the company.'*

- *The organisations who responded in a 'late, curt and rude' manner seem to be unaware that customer, public and shareholder relations, and communication are a vital part of their operation, and play an important part in generating the regard in which they are held publicly. It can take many years to build a reputation and only a few seconds to lose it – as the Ratner Group discovered (see case study 12.7).*

Remedial action
Adopt as a company external communication rule that all items of correspondence will be acknowledged within 24 hours and answered, where necessary, within 15 working days.

Internal commitment generates external benefits

A committed and well-briefed workforce, which cannot be achieved without adequate information and communication, can be incentivised and enthused. In turn customers' reactions can be considerably affected by the approach taken by the employees. Enthusiasm is infectious. The customer who sees that the employees are committed to, and enthusiastic about, the organisation and its products is far more likely to buy and to repeat buy than the customer who finds employee attitudes unenthusiastic, apathetic or even abusive. Employee attitudes act as a recommendation and positive endorsement.

Case study 16.6
MARK THIS

Lord Sieff, former chairman of Marks & Spencer, told the story of an assistant at one of that company's stores who wrote to him that she felt the range in the store was poor, as within five minutes she had to refuse three customers. 'It's not good enough', she wrote to her chairman, 'we get customers coming from [a considerable] distance'.

As a result of her action, the company improved the range at her store, and the sales increase was immediate and considerable.

Key technique
The sales assistant was committed to her company, partly it must be assumed because she responded to the company's well-known policy of commitment to its staff. She wrote to the chairman since she believed he needed to know and would welcome knowing. The ethos of the organisation suggested an action. As a result the customers were pleased, so was the assistant and so, no doubt, were the company's shareholders. The ethos of that organisation – a great communicator in its own right – encouraged the employee to respond to a problem.

211

Speak up

Encouraging employees to speak up is essential to achieve great communication. Those at the sharp end who are encouraged to do so often have a greater understanding of the problems than those responsible, but perhaps distant from the day-to-day requirements. This is the essence of the suggestion scheme concept addressed earlier, but it can work in other ways.

Case study 16.7
UP THE POLE

Formal suggestion schemes work on the basis that employees are encouraged to think of ideas on an individual basis. However, greater creativity may be encouraged by means of brainstorming sessions, which, while costly in time, can be very positive. Pacific Power and Light (PP&L) is an American power supply company which operates in some rough conditions in the north-west USA. In many of the mountainous areas power is transmitted on overhead lines which often break under the weight of accumulated ice formed by the freezing of the constant snow. The method of avoiding breakages was to send linesmen along the line with poles, constantly knocking the snow off before it froze. Several brainstorming sessions with the linesmen were held to try and solve this problem, during one of which a linesman complained that the previous week he had been chased by a bear. The suggestion was then made that if they could get the bears to climb the poles the weight of the animal would shake the snow off the lines. This in turn led to a suggestion that the company should put honey pots on top of the poles to induce the bears to climb them. The problem of how to place the honey pots on top of the poles then arose and the use of a helicopter was suggested. Cutting across this fanciful and increasingly risible idea came the notion that the downdraught from the helicopter rotors would itself remove the snow before it froze. Nowadays PP&L use the downdraught from overflying helicopters to clear their lines.

Key technique
Perhaps only a few companies would have allowed a meeting of their staff, addressing the serious problem of change, to apparently go off on the fanciful tangent of encouraging bears to go after honey pots at the top of power poles, and yet it was only because they had gone through that idea that the eventual solution was discovered.

The right message for the right audience

As can be seen from case study 16.7, communication can take many forms and generate positive contributions. However, the message must be correctly fashioned otherwise the reverse can be true. Irrespective of whether we are dealing with an internal or external audience we need to consider both the message itself and the target audience. We need to ensure our message is clear and unambiguous – and that it is a message appropriate to the audience blessed with its receipt. Often both these essential aspects can be overlooked.

Case study 16.8
RIPE FOR A RUDE RETORT

In August 1994 the *Financial Times* published an extract from a letter from a leading clearing bank which read 'Dear Sir, We hereby give you notice that by retrocession dated 2nd August 1994 [name of bank] have retrocessed, reponed and restored . . .'. 'Repone' is not listed at all in my several dictionaries, while 'retrocession' seems to mean 'cede back again'. To achieve some basic communication with the external addressee of the letter, the bank would be better advised to use ordinary English. The words might be capable of being used internally where at least the recipient could ask the author what he or she means.

Key technique
It is worth repeating a point already made – basically if the recipient fails to understand the message:

- *it is the fault and responsibility of the author; and*

- *communication cannot take place which completely negates the whole point of the exercise.*

213

Case study 16.9
MISSED THE TARGET

During the 1980s the incidence of skin cancer apparently caused by the effects of sunshine increased rapidly – by over 40,000 cases claimed one newspaper. In one Surrey hospital those needing to be admitted for a minor, but painful operation, to alleviate the effects of this disease, were required to wait in a dingy waiting room, the depressive nature of which was 'enhanced' by the posting of several notices warning of the effects of unprotected sunbathing. The patients, most of whom were in an apprehensive frame of mind as they anticipated their operations, thus received no comfort from their surroundings, but merely an entirely pointless and irritating reminder of how they came to be there.

Key technique
The messages of the posters were being aimed at the wrong audience – literally preaching to the converted. The only people in the waiting room were sufferers who well knew (albeit too late – for which they might have felt like criticising the medical profession for only issuing their warnings after the event) the dangers the posters sought to warn against.

It is said that the Medes and Persians always made decisions twice –
once when drunk and once when sober. In trying to communicate well
– to become a great communicator – perhaps we would be well advised
to follow their example, not necessarily meaning that we need to
become half-cut before taking an initial decision, but that we need to
think carefully of our message, of the means we use to convey it, of the
needs of the target audience and their likely reaction (and even our
reaction to their reaction) before we commence its construction. Even
then that is only the tip of the iceberg, as by far the greater challenge
is listening to the response and generating progress as a result.

Communicating effectively is not something that can be lightly – or
even easily – achieved. Becoming a great communicator is a task that
needs plenty of practice, and a determination that when we get it
wrong we recognise the failing and learn from it. For heaven's sake –
get out there, communicate and lead.

If, as the CBI stated, 'effective communication with employees is one
of the major issues facing management over this decade', the challenge
for the leaders of our organisations is already upon us. We need more
of our organisations' leaders to become great communicators – to generate pride, inspiration and enthusiasm. We need our leaders out there
at the sharp end on the shop floor, leading from the front, talking to and
listening to, and above all communicating with to generate communication from their employees – the people they want to make things
happen. Their example in turn should help us all become great communicators or at least improve our efforts in meeting the challenge. In
short we need those responsible for directing their organisation's
activities to lead and to give a lead from the front – like Henry V.
Perhaps the war will not be as lengthy or the battle as close fought as
Agincourt, but the stakes in terms of the survival and profitability of
our organisations are as keen.

An holistic view

Becoming a great communicator should be personally satisfying.
Indeed some may even see it as an end in itself. However, while it may
be an achievement, it is far more beneficial (and cost-effective) if seen
and used as a means to an end – bringing a benefit or improvement to
all those with whom we interface, as well as generally to the organisation within which we operate. Virtually automatically this will lead to

better rapport with, and understanding by, all involved – suppliers, customers, owners as well as employees – the original and essential target of the great (internal) communicator.

In relation to those it controls, good management can be said to have five main roles – to **L**isten, to **E**ncourage, to **A**dvise and to **D**elegate. The fifth, and by far the most important, role is made up of the initial letters of the first four – to L E A D. Management is all about leadership. As the head of Hewlett Packard Europe said recently 'you manage processes, but you lead human beings'. We cannot lead unless we communicate – 'he who communicates, leads'. Sadly, with some notable exceptions, it seems that, currently, in virtually every walk of life, politics, royalty, sport and business, real positive leadership in the UK is a rare attribute. The solution is simple – the challenge of effective leadership is the challenge of meaningful communication.

Further Contacts

■

Institute of Personnel and Development, IPD House, Camp Rd., Wimbledon, London SW19 4UX (0181-946 9100)

MORI, Human Resource Research, 95 Southwark Street, London SE1 0HX (0171-928 5955)

Research Services Ltd, RSL House, Elmgrove Road, Harrow, Middlesex HA1 2QG (0181-861 6000)

Industrial Society, Robert Hyde House, 48 Bryanston Square, London W1H 7LN (Cascade briefing groups introduction, Effective leadership courses, etc.) (0171-262 2401)

United Kingdom Association of Suggestion Schemes, PO Box 55, Wetherby, West Yorkshire

British Association of Industrial Editors (Communicators in Industry), 3 Locks Yard, High Street, Sevenoaks, Kent TN13 1LT (01732 459331)

Bibliography

■

Politics and the English Language, George Orwell.

Employee communication and consultation, (ACAS).

Making it happen, Sir John Harvey Jones, Collins, 1988.

Managing to survive, Sir John Harvey Jones, Collins, 1993.

Managing your internal customers, Kevin Thompson with Kathy Whitwell, *Financial Times*/Pitman Publishing, 1993.

ONE STOP Personnel Management, David M. Martin, ICSA Publishing, 1992.

How to control your costs and increase your profits, David M. Martin, Directors Books, 1992.

Wake up and shake up your company, Richard Koch and Andrew Campbell, *Financial Times*/Pitman Publishing, 1993.

Monty – The battles of Field Marshal Montgomery, Nigel Hamilton, Hodder & Stoughton, 1994.

Piercing the Atlantic Wall, Robert J. Kershaw, Ian Allan, 1994.

Management Kinetics, Carl Duerr, McGraw Hill, 1971.

Psychology – general, industrial, social, John Munro Fraser, Pitman Publishing, 1963.

Corporate communication for managers, Peter Jackson, Pitman Publishing, 1987.

The nice company, Tom Lloyd, Bloomsbury, 1990.

How to run suggestion schemes successfully, (available from Industrial Society, Robert Hyde House, 48 Bryanston Square, London W1H 7LN (0171-262 2401).

Empowerment: what organisations really do, (available from Harbridge House Consulting Group, 3 Hanover Square, London W1R 9RD (0171-629 6341).

Index

■